MONU-MENTAL
ABOUT
Prehistoric Dublin

MONU-MENTAL ABOUT
ABOUT
Prehistoric Dublin

TOM FOURWINDS

NONSUCH

*To Tracey, who would have loved these sites
even more than I do. We miss you!*

First published 2006

Nonsuch Publishing Limited
73 Lower Leeson Street
Dublin 2
Ireland
www.nonsuch-publishing.com

British Library Cataloguing in Publication Data.
A catalogue record for this book is available from the British Library.

ISBN 1 84588 560 0
ISBN-13 978 1 84588 560 1

Typesetting and origination by Tempus Publishing Limited
Printed in Great Britain

Contents

Forward at 45° – Location, Location, Location

Until relatively recent times, ancient monuments were viewed solely as isolated structures and their purpose was considered purely on the archaeological finds they yielded. It was observed early on that some sites might be aligned to certain solar events, such as the now well-known winter solstice sunrise alignment of the passage at Newgrange. Stone circles in particular were studied in this stellar-, solar- and lunar-event respect, mainly because no other purpose could be thought of for them (apart from Erik Von Daniken and T.C. Lethbridge proposing that they could have been landing-pads or beacons for extra-terrestrial visitors. The difference between the two propositions was that Lethbridge's book *The Sons of God: A Fantasy,* implied that he was simply toying with an idea, whereas Von Daniken stated it as being fact.) During these studies of stone circles it was also realised that many used significant landmarks to emphasise these alignments, but it seemed to stop there. Monuments were (and to a large extent still are) thought to have been placed almost randomly within the landscape. Several trends in location have long been commented on in the past, e.g. portal tombs are generally situated near running water, but again no real thought has gone into why these trends exist. If there is to be any progress in the understanding of these ancient wonders or the motives of their builders, it is necessary that the overall approach to their study be changed. To appreciate and analyse a site properly, it is not enough to simply revise this thinking, but also to totally reverse it: if any progress is to be made, then we must stop thinking that the monument is set in a 'ritual landscape' and realise that the actual landscape itself must be considered as part of the monument.

It is clear that these monuments took a great deal of time to construct and the effort involved tells us that they were extremely important to the Ancients who undertook their construction. Today we think in terms of modern urban conditions where we build things wherever there is a spare bit of land. If, as in more rural areas, there are larger areas available, we choose the position that best suits our needs: close to the road for easy access, away from the road but with a great view etc. A similar process must have been true for these monuments; they have not just been dropped randomly into the landscape, but placed in very special, carefully selected and (dare I say it) very sacred places.

Some of the reasons as to why certain places were special or sacred are forever lost to us, because we simply do not know, nor will we ever truly understand, the mind-sets of the Ancients. We can however, gain insight into their psyche through the physical evidence not only at, but also around the sites they left behind. As mentioned above, some are placed or constructed so that special solar, lunar or celestial events occur in a spectacular manner when viewed from the site. Others are located so that a particular hill or other landscape feature, presumably one that was held to be sacred, is visible 'just so' when you stand at a monument. In the case of hills, this may be that the peak of the hill is visible between two intervening hills or can be seen protruding above the false horizon created by nearer hills. These teasing alignments can only be seen after many visits to monuments within the vicinity and by observing trends in the landscape panoramas. Sometimes, however, a site was chosen so that the sacred hill simply dominates the monument and its presence is unambiguous, such as at Carrowmore in County Sligo.

Many monuments seem to be built on or near to rocky outcrops: places where the bedrock thrusts through the ground, often producing fantastically shaped formations. These are often noted in archaeological inventories, but their importance is rarely considered. Were these outcrops a convenient quarry for the building materials or were they of greater significance? If current speculation is correct and the Ancients were worshipers of Mother Earth, then it is possible that these rocky outcrops were a kind of proto-temple used before the tombs were built nearby. Just as so many churches are built on sites known to have been places of earlier pagan worship, a people who no longer had the beliefs held by those who worshipped at these rock formations, but knew them to have once been special places, may have built the tombs in a continuance of practice at old religious sites. The early Christian Church did not invent the practice of assimilating 'old religion' sites into the 'new religion'.

Although things are changing, when studying a monument many archaeologists count the stones and spend most of their time on their knees peering into the hole they have just dug in search of tangible evidence. There is a need to justify their funding to those who pay the bills, and the bill payers like nice, shiny brooches, stone axes and suchlike. Through close observation of a monument's landscape and acknowledging the surroundings as part of the monument itself, we can begin to see the wood for the trees. This is fieldwork beyond digging. It is something that does not produce tangible results such as axes, bowls and burials and so the commercial archaeological establishment is reluctant to undertake this work and this is where we, the enthusiasts and amateurs, enter the picture. It is up to us to visit these places and take note not only of the stones that form a structure, but also of the surrounding landscape. It is often very rewarding to remove oneself from a site and look at it from many angles and distances, in order to take in the 'bigger picture'. With the monument set into the landscape and not rearing up in front of you and dominating your view, more often than not, some of its secrets take shape before you.

Crockaunadreenagh,
County Dublin 2005

Introduction

For over 200 years now the antiquities of Ireland have come under a great deal of scrutiny, especially the older, pre-Christian monuments. This interest was originally part of a wider programme of research and investigations into the Celtic heritage of Ireland. For the first fifty years of the nineteenth century the scholars of Dublin were seemingly obsessed with translating the ancient manuscripts from Irish into English. In the 1830s efforts were undertaken to map the country, recording the exact townland boundaries and the positions of old churches and other monuments. Inhabitants of the various regions were questioned about the origins and meanings of place names, so that those mentioned in old manuscripts and legends could be identified. Possibly the greatest achievement of this cross-referencing work was the identification of The Hill of Tara and that of Brú na Bóinne, Newgrange by John O'Donovan, who worked with George Petrie at the Dublin based Ordnance Survey of Ireland.

The majority of people who undertook this work were not archaeologically trained scholars, because at this time the discipline of archaeology was not a formal one – these were the original antiquarians. The majority of these people were from the landed, upper classes and so mainly of English extraction, and as can be expected from an occupying nation, these scholars were totally unwilling to acknowledge the possibility that the indigenous population could have built monuments such as Newgrange. In fact they credited the building of Newgrange to the Danes – an error of a mere 4,500 years or so. This trend of denial, amazingly, remained until recent times, and to an extent still exists today, as we will see in the discussion on passage tombs below.

Some of the earliest theories were more adventurous though. These include such suggestions as that places like Newgrange were sun temples and that rock art was more than random groupings of simple motifs – some went as far as saying that the carvings in the Boyne Valley represented celestial objects and events. However, these 'unorthodox' theories were shunned and soon forgotten by the establishment. Ironically, many of these theories were to re-emerge in recent times, often without any knowledge of the earlier proposals, and again be denounced as rubbish by sections of the archaeological fraternity.

Serious scientific excavations commenced in the early twentieth century. Until this time many monuments had been ransacked, often in the name of excavation by the people alleged to be studying them, and a great deal of information was lost through their poor methods, which usually just involved hiring a few local people and getting them to dig a big hole. The more calculated approach that followed led to a far greater, but still incomplete, awareness of the lives of the people that built these structures. The findings of these investigations were published in archaeological papers and were not made readily available to the public. The middle of the twentieth century would see this change.

Books with titles like *Prehistoric Ireland* (Rafferty, 1951) began to appear. These were general discussions on the findings of excavations, which tried to put them into some form of context. As current thinking changed books went out of publication and new ones appeared and comparing their theories and thoughts today makes for very interesting reading. These books were, however, still of little interest to anyone outside the archaeological establishment due to the academic style usually adopted.

In the 1960s the situation changed when Estyn Evans published *Prehistoric And Early Christian Ireland – A Guide*. This not only discussed Irish history and prehistory but also had a gazetteer of sites. This somewhat limited gazetteer not only gave details of sites but also gave positional information in the form of grid references using the National Grid. For the first time it was possible for anyone with an interest to go out and visit some of the more 'off the beaten track' monuments. Unfortunately, this book quickly disappeared from print, but still appears in many bibliographies to this day. In 1980, Anthony Weir published *Early Ireland – A Field Guide*, which expands upon Evans' earlier work. *Early Ireland* had a very limited publication size and was, sadly, never reprinted. Although both of these titles are still useful books, republishing them would not be a viable option; information and attitudes towards the various monuments and the people who built them have changed so much that the front essay section would need to be completely rewritten. When these books were written, sites had to be located through reading archaeological papers and reports and then visited with the navigational help of local people, whereas today we have the Ordnance Survey maps to guide us. This means that relatively few sites feature in the gazetteer sections of these titles and these would now need a considerable amount of work to bring them up to date.

The 1980s and early 1990s saw a gamut of New Age type books, the majority of which contained little substance and a lot of speculation. The bulk of these seemed to be pandering to a readership that wanted fantasy and magic to be real, as well as clinging to the hope that a universal Mother Goddess once existed. Fortunately, this trend has subsided and books of a more serious tone have prevailed, but the gazetteer-style book is still poorly represented. One exception to this is Cary Meehan's *Sacred Ireland*, a well produced guide to many sites across Ireland. Quite amazingly, though, it does not contain a single entry for County Dublin, which has always been poorly represented in this field.

With the vast majority of people living in and around Dublin, it seems a little odd that interesting places on their doorstep are not made more accessible to them. People lead such busy lifestyles nowadays that they rarely have the time or energy to travel to opposite sides of the country for a Sunday day trip. With this in mind it is hoped that this book will show the people of Dublin the wealth of historical attractions that lies within their own county.

There is no shortage of general guidebooks featuring both megalithic and early Christian sites throughout greater Ireland. Undoubtedly, counties such as Cork, Sligo and Kerry have some of the best monuments and certainly have very high concentrations of them, but this is not much use to people living in Dublin who want to take a day trip on a Sunday afternoon. It is for these 'day trippers' who wish to find something new to visit, that this book is written as much as for the hardened megalithic enthusiast.

Since setting up a website (www.megalithomania.com) dedicated to the antiquities of Ireland, the author has received many emails thanking him for alerting people to the many sites that the east coast has to offer, in particular those in and around County Dublin. It is ultimately these comments that have led to this book being written.

Throughout the text you will come across assertions and comments as well as some facts and figures. Sources have not been provided in the body of the text to keep the size of the book as small as possible, and because footnotes and endnotes tend to break up the flow of reading. A bibliography of the works referred to and for recommended reading, can be found at the rear of the book. Some of these are academic works, which can be quite difficult to read, and several are now out of print, but can easily be obtained via second-hand bookstores on the Internet.

Sites mentioned in the text that appear in ***bold italics*** feature in the gazetteer section.

Today's modern county boundaries meant little, if anything at all, to the builders of the prehistoric monuments; the few exceptions may be where a large natural feature such as a river forms a partial border between two counties. This presents us with a dilemma, because it is not possible to discuss many of the sites around the periphery of the county without considering nearby sites that are in neighbouring counties. This means that some sites mentioned in the text will not be in the gazetteer section because they are in County Meath, Kildare or Wicklow. Other sites further afield will also get a mention for the purposes of comparison. All of these site names appear in normal script.

A Tour of County Dublin

I live my best in the landscape, being at ease there;
the only trouble I find I have brought in my hand.
'The Rams Horn' – John Hewitt

When looking down from the summit of Three Rocks Mountain onto the sprawling conurbation of the city of Dublin, it is extremely difficult to try and picture what it would have looked like 200 years ago, to say nothing of 5,000 years ago. Where we now see housing estates, commercial buildings and tower cranes dominating the view, we once may have seen a swathe of green treetops punctuated by small clearings and divided by the River Liffey as it made its way across the plains after the long journey from high in the Wicklow Mountains to the sea. The two pictures could not be more different.

Lambay, Ireland's Eye and Howth would all have been offshore islands and perhaps seen as embodiments of a sacred threesome. The mountains would have looked considerably different too. Today the peaks are shrouded by peat bogs, but in 3000 BCE the climate was milder and the hilltops were more fertile places. The monuments on the summits that stand out so clearly today would have been even more prominent without the thick layers of peat. Erected as close to the heavens as possible, passage tombs such as those at *Ticknock* on Two Rocks Mountain and *Seahan,* would have dominated the skylines, especially when they were first constructed. The light grey moss-free stones of the cairns, perhaps interspersed with pieces of white quartz, would have caused them to shine out in contrast to the green of the hills.

However, not all the ancient monuments were built to be this conspicuous. Amongst the trees on the slopes below, across the plain and along the coast, many other monuments were built tucked away from sight in settings that inspired the romanticism of the eighteenth and nineteenth century antiquarians and their images of white-clad Druids lurking in groves, sacrificing virgins on the capstones of dolmens that will forever be referred to by many as 'Druids' Altars'.

Lambay and Ireland's Eye from Howth

Other tomb types have also been given colloquial names. Wedge tombs are often referred to as 'The Giant's Grave' or 'Dermot and Graine's Bed', while an early reference to *Ticknock* passage tomb on Two Rocks Mountain called it a 'Cave' – a reference to the then exposed passage that has since collapsed and become hidden.

The *Ticknock* passage tomb, known locally as the Fairy Castle, is not the only monument to have changed since the 1800s. Moving down the south-western slopes of Two Rocks Mountain, we come to the wedge tomb in *Ballyedmonduff* townland (TD). Sketches made at the time of the 1830s Ordnance Survey show the grass-covered cairn reaching the tops of the wall stones with at least one roof stone in place. A very different picture greets the visitor today. Following excavation in 1945, which uncovered Beaker pottery and several flint tools dating the monument to around 2000 BCE, the monument was rebuilt in such a way that a visitor from the 1830s would hardly recognise it. On the northern slopes of Kilmashogue Mountain in *Kilmashogue* TD, there is another wedge tomb that is in an even sorrier state. Many of the gallery wall stones or orthostats have been removed along with much of the kerb that surrounds the denuded cairn. Set into the cairn, behind the gallery, are two later cist burials one of which has its capstone displaced slightly, allowing you to see inside.

Further down the slopes we come to two portal tombs, one also in *Kilmashogue* TD and another in *Taylorsgrange*, known as 'The Brehon's Chair'. Taking several

Kilmashogue portal tomb in Larch Hill Scout Camp

standing stones that are also in the vicinity of these tombs we already have a surprising number of monuments, and we haven't even gone further than the first
cluster of hills!

In the next three sections I will discuss the monuments of County Dublin by
approaching them in three separate groups: the Dublin Mountain sites, the coastal
sites and the sites of the main plane. As the first two are geographically contained in
a strip, they are presented as a trip from one end to the other. The latter group is discussed as a whole. Because I have to draw a line somewhere to separate the sections,
I have used major roads as boundaries – they are after all as artificial and meaning-
less as modern county boundaries when considering ancient monuments and their
landscapes. The first covers everything in the region south of the M50 as far as junction 11 with the N81 Blessington Road, then along the N81 until it reaches the N82
and then along the N7 to the Kildare border. The western edge of the coastal strip is
formed by the N11 and the M1. Everything else falls into the final section.

If you are unfamiliar with the differences between the various types of megalithic monuments, you may wish to read the monument descriptions that precede
the gazetteer section before continuing (page 51).

While reading the following sections you may wonder why you've never heard
of the sites mentioned. Amazingly, or rather unbelievably, only three of them have
an information board and not one of Dublin's monuments is signposted!

The Dublin Mountains and Their Foothills

If we journey inland starting on the coast at the Dublin/Wicklow border between Shankhill and Bray, the first high ground we encounter is Carrickgollogan Mountain with its bare, bulbous pinnacle. A hand-drawn map in the Dublin Ordnance Survey Letters shows many cairns and mounds around the top of the peak. Now only one monument survives, in **Carrickgollogan** TD, and this is in such a poor state of repair it is uncertain whether it is a portal or a wedge tomb.

In 1998, during the laying of a gas pipeline from Carrickmines to Bray, a wedge tomb was discovered in Shankhill TD on the east side of Carrickgollogan. This has a 2.35m long gallery, with an east-facing entrance comparable to the wedge tombs at **Laughanstown** and **Carrickgollogan**. The site was reburied. Shankhill also had a portal tomb that has long since been destroyed, but was thankfully drawn by George Petrie.

Continuing west we pass by The Scalp and the sites of many monuments that have now disappeared and we come to the foothills proper of the Dublin Mountains. In **Ballybetagh** TD to the east of Glencullen village, there are the remains of several cairns which possibly belong more to the group of coastal monuments which will be discussed later. The area around Glencullen must have been very special in prehistoric times. Even though a large number of monuments have been destroyed, there is still a wealth of sites to see.

On **Newtown Hill** above Johnny Fox's Pub, there is a very nice barrow, a standing stone, a cashel or stone fort, a cairn known as Oissin's Grave and the remains of stone circles. To the west of the barrow and standing stone there is a possible stone row. Two stones, each 1m tall, align with the Great Sugar Loaf Mountain, 9km away in County Wicklow. A third stone, that may have been part of the row, lies at the base of the southern stone. **Glencullen's** real treasure is to be found in the valley below, on the golf course opposite the pub – a beautiful standing stone of solid quartz known as 'Queen Mab'. The monuments missing from the area include another quartz standing stone known as 'The Stone of the Hound' and a small tomb in Ballybrack TD to the north of Newtown Hill, which was destroyed around 1860.

The destroyed tomb at Shankhill

'Queen Mab' in Glencullen

The lost tomb at Ballybrack near Glencullen

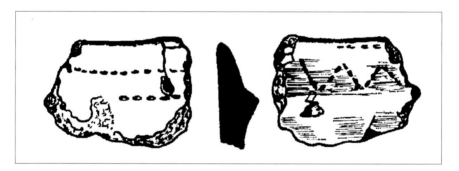

Pottery found at Kiltiernan Domain. *(After Herity)*

One mile north of Newtown Hill stands one of Ireland's largest portal tombs in **Kiltiernan Domain** TD. Aptly described by Borlase as 'a sphinx-like monster, advancing out of a rocky hill on some half-dozen short and rickety legs', the huge capstone is held aloft by relatively tiny stones, giving the impression of a prowling beast lurking in the gorse. When a concrete pillar was put in place in 1956 to help support the capstone, small-scale excavations were undertaken that uncovered Coarse Ware Neolithic pottery. At 7.5m long and weighing in at an estimated 40 tons, the capstone is amongst the largest in Europe.

From Glencullen we start to climb into the mountains, passing **Ballyedmonduff** wedge tomb mentioned above, along the way. Extensive excavation of this wedge

The tors on Three Rocks Mountain

tomb took place in 1945 by two of the great names amongst Irish archaeologists: Séan P. Ó Ríordáin and Ruaidhrí de Valéra. Finds included a polished hammer with an hourglass-shaped perforation, a possible polishing stone, a flint scraper, fragments of Beaker and Coarse Ware pottery. One of the stones in the cairn has seven cup marks. Photographs taken at the time of excavation, when pine trees did not surround and smother the tomb, show that the tors on the southern end of Two Rocks Mountain are clearly visible from the tomb and appear on the false summit.

Underneath the radio and television masts on **Three Rocks Mountain**, are the three granite tors that lend the mountain its name. The centre one of these has three bullauns in its upper surface, two of which may have been enhanced. These prompted Gabriel Beranger, an eighteenth-century antiquarian, to speculate that the tors may once have been used as sacrificial altars:

This mountain has on its summit three huge heaps of rock, piled one on another, and seen at some miles distance, from which the mountain takes its name. I take them to be altars on which sacrifices were offered … I have copied every stone as they are fixed, and the regularity which is observed in piling them convinces me that they are the work of man, as they could not grow in that position… The extensive summit of this mountain, the parched ground and its solitude, make it the most awful spot I had ever seen.

I wonder what he would say if he saw the hilltop today with all those masts! The tors are obviously natural formations and not 'the work of man' as Beranger speculated, but this does not mean that they were never the centre of ritual activity. They could have been 'proto-temples' used by pre-Neolithic societies. Beranger's comments mentioned a fourth, larger basin, which, from his description, resembled the ones found in the granite tors on Dartmoor, England. Two possible conclusions that can be drawn from this are that the basins are natural, as they occur in the same kind of geological feature, or there was a cultural/religious link between the two very distant areas. If the latter were the case then you would expect some of the other Dartmoor-typical monuments, such as long stone rows, to also be present in the area of Three Rocks Mountain. These are certainly not visible, but may lie buried beneath the peat.

From the top of Three Rocks Mountain the tracks west take us below the peak of Two Rocks Mountain, where the **Ticknock** passage tomb is, and on to Kilmashogue Mountain. Apart from the wedge tomb in **Kilmashogue** TD, mentioned above, there is a possible standing stone on the northern slopes. H. E. Kilbride-Jones excavated the wedge tomb in the 1950s, aided by de Valera and Ó Nualláin. The gallery has triple-walling, that is to say that the walls are each made of three rows of orthostats rather than the more normal two used in wedge tombs, and an antechamber opening to the west, facing the passage tombs on Montpelier. The excavation uncovered two Bronze Age cists burials inserted into the cairn and a third in the antechamber. All three cists contained cremations accompanied by an urn.

There are three portal tombs arranged around the base of Kilmashogue Mountain in **Taylorsgrange**, **Kilmashogue** and **Mount Venus** townlands.

All that remains of 'The Brehon's Chair' portal tomb at **Taylorsgrange** are the two 3m tall portal stones and the full-height door stone between them. Brehon is another word for a Druidical priest. The scale of these remains indicates that this tomb would have rivalled the largest portal tombs in the country. In 1985, prior to the construction of the M50 which now passes just metres from the tomb, the area surrounding the tomb was excavated and traces of habitation were uncovered, including postholes and pits. A secondary burial comprising a food vessel and cremated bones was discovered, along with traces of flint working. Further excavations in 1987 uncovered some interesting features that may have been pyre sites.

Kilmashogue portal tomb, which is located in the grounds of Larch Hill Scout Camp, is in bad repair. One portal stone and part of the chamber are still standing, the capstone leans against the sole upright chamber wallstone and the rest of the structure lies around them. The design of this monument is extremely similar to Onagh/Glaskenny portal tomb in the hills above Enniskerry, County Wicklow, but it does have one distinguishing feature – the remaining portal stone is set at right-angles to the chamber axis and there is a ground-level sill stone rather than

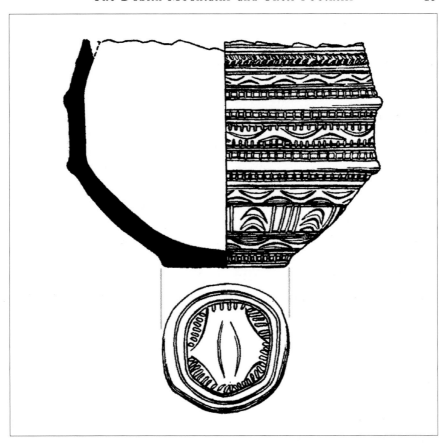

Middle Bronze Age food vessel found at Kilmashogue. *(After Ó Ríordáin)*

a door stone. The symmetry of portal tomb construction makes it safe to assume that the other portal stone, which now lies below the roots of a nearby tree, was set in a similar fashion. This portal stone arrangement can also be seen at the diminutive example in Ballyquin TD, County Waterford.

The **Mount Venus** tomb is a real oddball. It does not have a chamber as such; the massive capstone is held at a steep angle by a single portal stone, while the lower edge rests directly on the ground rather than on stones forming a chamber. There is also a standing stone and a stone row in **Kilmashogue** TD. The posts of several gateways in the wall alongside the road to Rockbrook, have a similar size and shape to those in the row and may have originally been taken from here.

The next peak is Tibradden Mountain and from here onwards it gets really busy. **Tibradden** itself now has a lone cairn that was excavated in 1850 and a stone-lined cist was discovered containing a food vessel and cremated bones, which now rest at the National Museum on Kildare Street, Dublin. For many years it was considered to be a passage tomb, but in 1956 conservation work revealed that

Looking south over Tibradden cairn

the open central area of the cairn was not an original feature, nor was the slender passage leading to the outside of the cairn. It had been speculated that this north-east facing passage had an ancient summer solstice alignment, but these claims are obviously made without knowledge of the 1956 findings. The whole hilltop of Tibradden is dotted with lumps and bumps which may be other peat-covered cairns or other contemporary features.

One of south Dublin's defining features is The Hell Fire Club, a ruined hunting lodge, on **Montpelier**, an isolated hill at the extreme north of the Dublin Mountains. This building was constructed using the cairn material from two passage tombs that stood to the rear of where the building was erected. A standing stone from the hilltop was also used. It is still just possible to see where one of the tombs was situated, from very subtle circular earthworks to one side of the building with a dip at the centre, which is presumably where the chamber was. The Ordnance Survey trig point stands on one edge of it. Behind the building is a much larger mound. On the southern side of the badly damaged mound, which is still up to 1.5m tall in places, are four visible kerbstones and two buried ones can be detected below the grass. A mere 100m to the south-west there is a small, fallen standing stone.

On the eastern slopes of the hill there is another standing stone and in the valley between Montpelier and Cruagh Mountain there is a small wedge tomb in **Killakee** TD that has many similarities to **Ballyedmonduff** wedge tomb. This was first recorded as recently as 1978 by Paddy Healy, which just shows that

Knockanteedan from the south-east

there may still be a lot to be discovered even within a few miles of Ireland's capital.

Montpelier guards the entrance to the Glenasmole Valley; an area rich in history and folklore. Here the River Dodder flows down from the Dublin Mountains on its way to meet the Liffey at Ringsend. The majority of the monuments here are on the eastern slopes of the valley. Near to the entrance of the valley, tucked into the corner of a field on the top of a steep slope overlooking the dam of the lower reservoir, there is a denuded mound called Knockanteedan (the little hill of the blasts) in **Glassamucky** TD. One side of the mound is covered in gorse bushes and the top has been dug away making it look rather forlorn now.

Two kilometres up the valley on the slopes above the upper reservoir, the ruins of St Anne's Church stand on another mound, which may be prehistoric. Halfway between the two, on the opposite side of the reservoirs, there is another possible mound. This is so similar to the mound that St Anne's Church stands on, that they are both either natural or man-made. It is said that St Anne's gets its name from St Sentan who is supposed to have founded the site. It is just possible that the name derives from Ainne, one of the female goddesses who may have been worshiped here in pre-Christian times.

High above the church in **Piperstown** TD, lie the remains of a whole complex of sites, including a stone circle, cairns, hut sites and standing stones. The stony nature of the hilltop makes it extremely difficult to find these structures on the ground. These were first noticed after a fire burnt away the peat covering in 1960. Etienne Rynne and Patrick Healy excavated and recorded the complex in 1962.

Roughly 1000m up the valley from the Piperstown monuments there is another stone circle in **Glassamucky Brakes** TD. This is very hard to locate as the whole hillside around it is strewn with boulders. Below the circle across the road are the remains of some more hut sites of undetermined age.

There is a small portal tomb in **Cunard** TD, near to the head of the Glenasmole Valley. This is built on a fast-flowing stream on a small rise above a waterfall. The platform, on which the tomb is constructed, seems to be an outcrop of different rock to the granite that surrounds it. On the rock-strewn slopes above the Cunard portal tomb there is a possible stone row, also in **Cunard** TD. This comprises of three stones each about 20m from the next, aligned south-west to north-east. Its south-western end terminates at a round platform beside the same stream as the portal tomb.

High above Cunard, where the Dublin/Wicklow border makes a sharp turn on **Glassamucky Mountain**, is a fine bullaun stone. From this stone I have observed the winter solstice sun rising to one side of the Great Sugarloaf Mountain, the peak of which protrudes just above the false horizon created by the hills in between. A flat-topped rock a few metres from the bullaun stone has a line of long cup marks in its upper surface. Markings similar to these are found on stones in many of the Wicklow/Kildare stone circles, on the stone separating the two chambers of **Ballyedmonduff** wedge tomb and also on the central tor at Three Rocks Mountain.

Compared to the eastern side of the valley, the west side is very sparsely populated by monuments, with none actually in the valley itself. At the north end, high above the lower reservoir, there is an overgrown barrow in the saddle between Carrigeenoura and Slievenabawnoge Mountains in **Ballinascorney Upper** TD. It is almost impossible to spot on the ground now, but its location makes the site worth visiting. The views to the west and north-west encompass many of the sites around **Knockanvinidee**, **Knockannavea** and on Saggart Hill, which we will come to soon. Of special interest is the way that the main mound on Knockanvinidee in **Ballymana** TD appears on the skyline just to one side of the slopes of Slievenabawnoge.

Two and a half kilometres to the south of Ballinascorney Upper TD, is **Seahan** Mountain. This is one of a group of three peaks that form their own group. Seefingan and Seefin both have monuments on their summits – a cairn and excellent passage tomb respectively – but these are both in County Wicklow and so are not covered by this book. When viewed from the Blessington Road near Brittas, the well-matched rounded peaks of Seefin and Seahan look like a pair of breasts, much like the Paps of Anu in County Cork, with the cairns on the summits polishing off the imagery perfectly. A large cairn and a passage tomb are the main attractions on the top of Seahan. The Seahan complex is the highest site in

Cunard portal tomb from the south-east

Dublin. At the centre of the main passage tomb's mound, the top of the roofstone of the chamber and one or two orthostats of the passage are visible.

Most reports mention a third monument, a ruined passage tomb that is to the south of the cairn. During a second visit to the hilltop during preparation for this book, I noticed a fourth, very ruined structure, deeply embedded in the peat to the north of the main passage tomb.

The R114 from Bohernabreena village to Brittas, separates Slievenabawnoge from Tallaght Hill, much of which is now covered in pine plantation. Next to the start of the cul-de-sac leading from the R114 to the car park beside the plantation, there is a very good example of a ring barrow in **Belgard Deer Park** TD. In the same townland, but on the other side of the road, there is also a possible stone circle. Near to the houses at the end of the road there is a large ring fort and the remains of a passage tomb in **Ballymaice** TD. The passage tomb looks out over the entrance to the Glenasmole Valley, and to the north-west Howth is a very prominent feature. Many of the sites across this section could have been placed here to mark the summer solstice sunrise above Howth.

The ringfort mentioned above could be of major importance. In the valley below lies the small village of Bohernabreena, which translates to Road of the Hostel. During the 1837 Ordnance Survey work, John O'Donovan identified this as possibly being the site of Da Derga's hostel made famous in the story of 'The Destruction of Da Derga's Hostel'. O'Donovan suggested that a different ringfort near to Bohernabreena was the site of the hostel, but as Henry Morris pointed

Looking towards Howth from Ballymaice passage tomb

out the place name indicates that the hostel was elsewhere. Could it be the one further up the valley on the top near to Knockanvinidee? The rich wealth of other monuments in the immediate vicinity certainly indicates that it was once a very important location.

The modern Ordnance Survey map shows just three monuments in **Ballymana** TD: the ringfort, the passage tomb and a mound called **Knockanvinidee**. However, the hill has many more sites including a possible stone circle, a cairn known as **Crookan Cairn** and the remains of a possible portal tomb. **Crookan Cairn**, the most interesting site on Saggart Hill, is just 50m west of the large mound. It is oval in plan with a fine kerb of large stones. The east end is marked by the largest stone in the kerb which has a sloping-outward facing with a thin layer of quartz covering it. This stone points directly towards Howth. The possible stone circle lies on the edge of a new pine plantation 100m north-west of **Crookan Cairn**. Just four low stones remain now amongst a collection of rusting cars.

Near to the highest point of this group of hills there is a large cairn called **Knockannavea**, which can easily be located by heading towards the radio aerials that stand next to it. Although this site is usually surrounded by pine trees, there are spectacular views to be had when these are cleared. To the south Black Hill, **Seahan** and Seefin dominate the landscape, with the cairns on the latter two clearly visible.

On the northernmost tip of Tallaght Hill is Lugmore TD. Here there is a fine open megalithic kist, which is one of the few to still have its capstone nearby. The chamber itself is approximately 1m long, 75cm wide and 1m deep. The overturned

Crookan Cairn with Howth in the distance

capstone lies to one side. The long axis of the cist points directly at **Knockannavea** cairn – although you cannot see the cairn from here due to intervening trees, but you can see the aerials mentioned above.

There are two townlands in this area with 'Lug' in their name: Lugmore and Lugg (see below). In *Irish Place Names,* P. W. Joyce states that Lug means 'hollow', but most Lug-related places I have visited are hills. I believe these places have more to do with the worship of the 'Celtic' deity Lugh, who lends his name to the harvest festival of Lughnasa and to the Irish word for August – Lúnasa.

The western side of Tallaght Hill slopes gently down for several kilometres before plunging into the valley below, known as the Slade of Saggart. On the upper part of the more gentle slopes in **Mountseskin** TD there is an artificial mound, adjacent to which there was once a barrow cemetery that has since been ploughed away. A little further west there is a large ring barrow also in Mountseskin. This is over 25m in diameter and the shallow traces of the ditch around it can be clearly seen. The ditch would have been much deeper when the barrow was first constructed, but it has filled up over time as well as being partially ploughed away.

Lower down the slopes in **Raheen** TD there is a large standing stone with fifteen or so cup marks at the base of its southern face. This basic rock art is one of only three examples to be found in Dublin.

In **Boherboy** TD, 800m from the foot of Verschoyles Hill stands Adam and Eve, a pair of standing stones aligned east-west. The eastern stone is pointed while the

Raheen standing stone

western one has a flat top. This configuration is quite common amongst stone pairs and is often referred to as a male/female pairing, as can be seen from the local name given to the stones: Adam and Eve. In such pairs it is usually the more phallic, pointed one that is the male stone, but here for some reason it is the flat-topped one that is known as Adam. Perhaps the flat top represents the more broad-shouldered profile stereotypically associated with men, or maybe the switching of the male and female roles was an attempt by the Church to remove any phallic symbolism.

At the northern entrance to the valley, between Saggart Hill and Tallaght Hill/ Verschoyles Hill, there is a cairn in Crooksling TD. It is interesting to note that this is in a very similar position to the mound mentioned above in **Glassamucky** TD at the entrance to Glenasmole Valley, and they may have been built as or acted as lookout platforms to monitor the entrance to the valleys below them. On the opposite side of the valley a small knoll projects in a north-easterly direction from Saggart Hill. On the top of this projection in **Lugg** TD, a multi-phase henge was excavated in the 1950s prior to the commissioning of the surrounding pine plantation. Inside the outer bank and ditch, traces of a thus far unique timber structure were revealed. This consisted of a ring of postholes with an avenue of posts leading off. Between the ring of posts and the outer bank were some larger postholes – a single one and two pairs. The excavation report rather fancifully suggests that the pairs of upright posts may have supported crosspieces forming trilithons – wooden versions of those found at Stonehenge in Wiltshire, England.

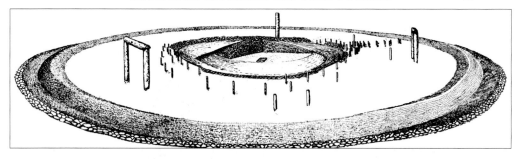

Reconstruction of the multi-phase monument. *(After H.E. Kilbride-Jones)*

The excavator, H. E. Kilbride-Jones, called this timber construction a 'sanctuary' structure, adopting the term coined by William Stukely to describe a monument not far from Avebury, again in Wiltshire. Within this structure were two hearths that each appear to have been ritually 'sealed' by placing a round pebble against the inside face of the westernmost wall-slabs.

After the timber structure had passed out of use, a small settlement was built on the site. The final stage saw the erection of the outer bank and ditch and the raising of the central barrow, in which two cremations were placed. The outer bank was faced with stone blocks. Today all that can be seen beneath the scrubby trees that infest the site are the outer and inner banks and ditches.

In the woods 250m to the north-east of this amazing monument, there is a chambered cairn, which could be the 'cairn called the moat of the hill of the burning' mentioned by Ball in 1920.

There is also a barrow cemetery on the southern slopes of Lugg, of which only one large barrow still exists. Ball also mentioned a mound in Glananareen TD known as Hungry Hill and a rath in Crooksling TD called The Place of the Kings, but none of these seem to be detectable.

The top of Saggart Hill has four monuments. At the northern end there is a cairn called Knockandinny and a ruined passage tomb in **Slievethoul** and **Crockaunadreenagh** TDs respectively. The large cairn has a smaller, almost indiscernible cairn butting up against it. The exposed orthostats of the passage tomb show that the passage was aligned slightly to the north of north-east, which rules out any summer solstice sunrise alignment. However, it does align with the passage tomb on the western side of Saggart Hill (see **Slievethoul** below). Six hundred metres to the north of these monuments, still in **Crockaunadreenagh** TD but not really on the hill, there is a barrow marked on the Ordnance Survey map. However, it is now either under a small pine plantation or was removed when the golf course was laid out. The cairn and passage tomb remains are separated by a modern field boundary, which also marks the border between the two townlands. The remaining orthostats of the passage tomb indicate that the passage aligned to the north-east, possibly marking the summer solstice sunrise. From the top of the cairn, on August 1st, the sun can be seen rising over the top of Lugg, adding weight to the possible association of the 'Lug' element in place names with the god Lugh.

On the southern peak of Saggart Hill, also in **Slievethoul** TD, amongst a mass of ugly aerials there is a seemingly unopened passage tomb. The top of this cairn has collapsed slightly showing where the chamber is, but this may actually be where the tomb has been opened at some time in the past and subsequently filled in. Two large stones on the west side of the mound may be displaced roofstones, and two boulders located 10m from the tomb could have served the same function or may perhaps be from the tomb's kerb. The mound is quite small, just 15m or so in diameter and 3.5m high. Unusually for passage tombs, neither this site nor the one at the north end of Saggart Hill occupy the highest points. There is, however, a third ruined passage tomb on the southern peak hidden in the trees. All that remains today is a 1m high, 25m diameter platform of rubble.

The Coastal Monuments

Again we start at the Wicklow/Dublin border between Shankill and Bray, but this time we travel north along the coast. Almost immediately we encounter a portal tomb in *Ballybrack* TD, which now stands on a green in front of The Cromlech Fields Housing Estate. With the top of the capstone measuring less than 2m in height, this is one of Ireland's smallest examples. Its small size means it has a very minimalist design, with just four small orthostats supporting the relatively over-sized capstone, which is a flat-bottomed split boulder. A small hole on one side of the capstone could be a deep cup mark or possibly where it was drilled in order to be blasted at some time. Similar holes can be found in some of the stones at the Druids' Judgment Seat in *Killiney* (see below). *Ballybrack* is one of the three Dublin monuments to have an information sign.

One of the most neglected and abused monuments in Dublin lies 2km inland in *Laughanstown* TD. This overgrown wedge tomb is just 50m from the junction of the M50 and Cherrywood spur. The tomb once stood on high ground and had wonderful views to the south, but now the new road is 30m higher than the tomb and all these views have been obstructed. Furthermore, it will soon be dwarfed by developments in the field to the north and all the views will be gone. Hopefully the concrete-filled red and white barrels that surround the site and the scrubby undergrowth that covers the mound, will be cleared up and good access to the site provided.

While the Cherrywood developments were being prepared, the proximity to both Tully church and the *Laughanstown* wedge tomb was sufficient to initiate many archaeological investigations seeking to assess the unseen remains in the area. The finds included several pits and hearths, but the most important discovery was a series of burials. A barrow, 8.5m in diameter and surrounded by a 60cm deep ditch, contained the skeleton of a child. At the centre of the mound there was a cremation burial. Close by in the mound was a circular stone setting containing five cattle teeth. The bottom of the encircling ditch was filled with charcoal and burnt bone, which is assumed to be the debris from the funeral pyre. One unusual and therefore

Left: Ballybrack portal tomb

Opposite above: Glendruid. Brennanstown portal tomb

Opposite below: Glendruid. An 1819 engraving made of a drawing by George Petrie

interesting feature was the discovery of struck flints that were mainly arranged at the four cardinal points. Other barrows were also identified in the area.

Excavations closer to the wedge tomb were undertaken prior to the construction of the Cherrywood spur, which runs shockingly close to the monument. They uncovered a 25m by 12m cairn, which contained flint arrowheads and pottery. Evidence of late prehistoric settlement was also discovered in the vicinity of the wedge tomb. The evidence gathered shows that this area has seen almost continuous occupation, starting in the Neolithic, through the Bronze Age and early Christian period to modern times.

Two ancient Christianised sites exist to the north of Laughanstown: Tully church and **Rathmichael** church. The latter is built inside a rath that was given to the church. Along the lane leading to the church, hidden in the undergrowth, there is an earthfast bullaun stone.

In stark contrast to the **Laughanstown** wedge tomb, one of Ireland's true heritage gems lies 1.5km north of **Laughanstown**: **Brennanstown** portal tomb, often referred to as Cabinteely dolmen or the more poetic Glendruid. Although restored and supported by a concrete arch, this is one of Ireland's finest monuments – far better than Poulnabrone portal tomb in The Burren, County Clare, for instance, which is one of the country's most photographed ancient monuments. With coach-loads of tourists visiting Poulnabrone daily it is hard to understand why **Brennanstown** (and **Kiltiernan Domain** for that matter) are not promoted more.

Brennanstown portal tomb has several features that make it unique: there is a small courtyard to the rear of the chamber and the massive capstone, estimated to weigh around 60 tons, has a channel carved into its upper surface. This acts like

Engraved by T.Dale & from a Drawing by Geo. Petrie for the Excursions through Ireland.

CROMLECH AT BRENNANSTOWN,
CO. OF DUBLIN.

Dalkey Island from the top of Dalkey Hill

a gutter, diverting rainwater to the sides of the capstone and preventing the rear courtyard from becoming sodden. The tomb stands alongside the northern spur of the Loughlinstown River, one of the tributaries of which rises 300m to the north of **Kiltiernan Domain** portal tomb.

In **Killiney**, 400m from the ruins of the old church, is one of the county's curios. Described in 1799 as 'three small cromlechs, surrounded by a circle of upright stones, about 135ft in circumference', The Druids' Judgment Seat is a Victorian folly built from the orthostats of the original monument. The stones forming the seat and several other orthostats, now stand in a small enclosure in the middle of a modern estate, but when it was first constructed the views would have been extensive. Sadly, nothing of the kerb mentioned in the quote above remains. A large cemetery of stone-lined graves 'with curious markings' were discovered nearby, which was possibly connected to the old church rather than the tomb. When the mound was opened around 1797, stone chambers containing skeletons and urns were found. With three tombs in a kerbed cairn or mound, this was a very special monument and its loss is a great one.

The obelisk on the top of **Dalkey Hill** is visible from much of south Dublin. Beneath it is a mound. Considering its position on a prominent hilltop and the fact that you can see loose rocks in places, it is almost certainly an ancient cairn and it would not be unreasonable to assume that it is actually a passage tomb. The obelisk has been fenced off because it is unsafe, but there are plans to renovate it. It would be nice if some time was given to investigate the true nature of the mound during this work.

In the sea below Dalkey Hill lies Dalkey Island, which has been inhabited off and on for 8,000 years. Early settlers would have used the tides to cross from the

Howth

continent and the Cornish and Welsh coasts. Before the use of motorised craft, traders and colonisers had to rely on winds and tides to plan their routes. In a discussion of tidal conditions in the Irish Channel, Margaret Davies identified three key Irish locations that are natural staging points on the Atlantic shipping route from the Straits of Gibraltar to the northern reaches of the British Isles. These are Waterford Bay in the south, Carlingford Lough in the north and Dublin Bay in the middle. The short crossing from Scotland to the north Antrim coast, may not have been the earliest route used to reach Ireland. Coastal fishermen from Cornwall straying too far from land could easily have found themselves being carried on by the prevailing tides to Dublin Bay.

Many parts of Dalkey Island were excavated in the late 1950s by various archaeologists. A mass of pottery covering many periods from the Neolithic through to medieval was found, as well as evidence of flint/chert working and bronze weapon casting in the form of crucibles and clay moulds. Other finds included hearths, a kiln, stone axes and polishing stones, bone pins, bronze brooches, beads and a fragment of Roman Samian ware. Amongst the Early Bronze Age burials excavated, one dating to 2300 BCE was found with its skull full of limpet shells. The report doesn't make it clear whether these had been placed there, indicating some kind of ritual activity, or had fallen inside from the nearby midden.

In front of the entrance to the walled churchyard at **Kill of the Grange**, 4.5km inland from Dalkey, there is a bullaun stone. This is a large boulder that has been tipped onto one side so that the only visible bullaun is now half buried.

Our next site is another of south Dublin's obelisks in **Stillorgan Park**. In 1955, a cist burial containing the remains of a woman was discovered beneath the mound on which the obelisk stands.

Nothing else of interest remains on the path of our northward journey until we leave the other side of the city itself and reach Howth. Once an island, Howth is now a promontory connected to the mainland by a strand at Sutton. In the annals it is given a very important place in Irish lore. The old name for Howth is Ben Edar or Benn Etair, which may be related to the sun goddess Etain.

There are a surprisingly large number of monuments on Howth, including a massive, partially collapsed portal tomb known as Aedeen's Grave in the rhododendron gardens of Howth Castle in **Howth Demesne** TD. Aedeen was the daughter of Aengus of Ben Edar. She is said to have died of grief at the loss of Oscar, her husband, in 284 CE – the tomb is obviously older than this date. Portal Tombs are more often than not associated with a stream or a river, but the nearest running water to the site is Bloody Stream some 500m to the east. However, landscaping works on the castle grounds may have removed any traces of a closer stream if it existed. Another unusual feature of this tomb is that the portal faces south, directly towards the face of Muck Rock 50m away. The capstone is estimated to weigh around 60 tons, making it the second largest in Ireland after Browne's Hill portal tomb (Co. Carlow), which is estimated to weigh around 100 tons.

On the top of Howth, overlooking the golf course, there are three cairns: two in **Blackheath** TD and one in **Dunhill** TD. Only one of the Blackheath cairns is exposed at the northern end of the Ben of Howth; the other is hidden beneath gorse and heather. Much of the cairn material has been removed over time, but the cist at its centre is visible. This is constructed from eight large stones rather than four slabs. On the top of Dunhill, three large kerbstones are all that remain of the cairn that once stood there. Nearby walkers have built small enclosures to act as windbreaks, which should not be mistaken for the cairn itself.

In **Sutton South** TD, still on Howth, there is a 4m high mound near to the sea. This is actually in the garden of a modern bungalow, but it can be seen from the beach if you know where to look. The rear wall of the garden has cut through the northern side of the tree-covered mound. In 1949 and 1970 a kitchen midden was excavated in Sutton. The second excavation was undertaken so that the age of the midden could be compared with the one discovered on Dalkey Island (see above). Through radiocarbon dating, the Sutton midden was dated to 3000 BCE, and it was concluded that they were contemporary. As at the Dalkey Island site, evidence of flintknapping came to light. A stone axehead was found during both of the Sutton excavations. Of the flint tools discovered, one was dated to the Mesolithic or possibly late Palaeolithic period.

On the highest part of the promontory, known as the Ben of Howth, there are three cairns. Two of these have exposed burial chambers. The flattened cairn at the north end of the Ben, above Muck Rock and Howth Demesne portal tomb, is positioned so that Lambay Island and Ireland's Eye line up with each other.

Back on the mainland in **Drumnigh** TD, 5km north-west of Howth, there is a rectangular, flat-topped mound. Standing on the top of this Howth dominates

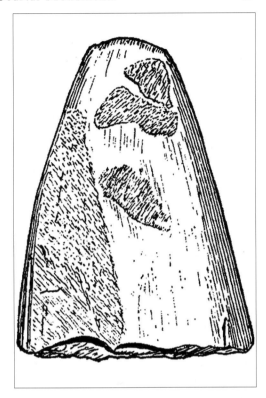

Stone axehead found at Sutton in
1970. *(After Mitchell)*

the south-eastern skyline and seems to loom as if it is much closer than it actually
is. There is a possible winter solstice sunrise alignment above Howth from this
site, which may have been the reason for its construction.

Between Drumnigh and Swords there is a raised area of land known as Feltrim
Hill. Extensive excavations took place here when it was under threat from quarrying, and they yielded fascinating results. As on Dalkey Island, evidence was
discovered that showed Mesolithic people had once used the hill. The hill was
also used for flintknapping, probably making use of flint nodules gathered on the
nearby beaches, as the nearest source of mineable flint is in north Antrim around
Mount Sandel. The excavations were initiated when flints and pottery were
discovered in spoil heaps at the quarry that was supplying hardcore for the construction of Dublin Airport. The digs covered large areas of the hilltop and many
interesting features were uncovered. The most interesting of these was a 'saucer
shaped depression', 16m in diameter, in which large quantities of worked flint
were discovered as well as masses of flint waste flakes, seven pieces of stone axe
and 300 sherds of pottery. It was concluded that this site was used by a flintknap-
per to finish tools. The axe pieces were mainly of andesite or greenstone, which
most likely came from Lambay Island (see below) or Portrane. One piece was
made of porcellanite from County Antrim, which shows that there was some

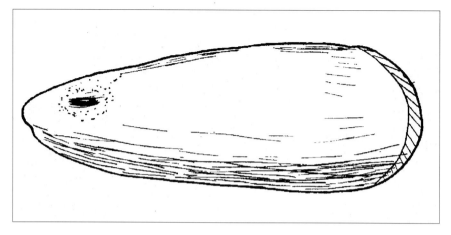

Stone axehead from Feltrim Hill. *(After Hartnett/Eogan)*

Decoration from the rims of potsherds found on Lambay. *(After Case)*

trade between Dublin and Antrim at this time. This trade link may indicate that the flint used here may also have come from Antrim.

On Lambay Island, which is privately owned, there is a great deal of prehistoric activity. As well as several cairns, it lays claim to one of the most important sites in County Dublin – a Neolithic axe factory. This is the only known such site where evidence of all stages of axe production has been found in the one location. As well as being quarried, the stone was carved into 'roughs' on site. It is more common for these to be taken elsewhere for final shaping and polishing, but polishing-stones were found at the axe factory. Large quantities of pottery were also found.

In Regles TD on the north-west edge of Lusk, there used to be a mound, but although this still appears on Ordnance Survey maps, no trace of it can be seen.

One kilometre north of Rush, in **Rush** TD, on the very edge of a cliff top overlooking Rush beach to the south, there is a single boulder that is all that remains of a passage tomb once known as Knocklea. This was once described as having

Balrothery church. Was it built on the site of an ancient monument?

a fine kerb and a cruciform chamber. Five hundred metres north in Drumanagh TD there is a large promontory fort defined by a large ditch and bank.

In **Knocken** TD just off the coast road, 1km north of Skerries, there is a cairn. This occupies the eastern end of a ridge that runs parallel to the coast. Not much of the monument exists today, but what does remain can be seen from the road at the base of the driveway to the adjacent farm.

Just under 2km inland from here there is a standing stone in **Balrothery** TD. As recently as 2001 this stone stood in a field on the east edge of the village, but it is now an unlikely centrepiece on a green surrounded by a new estate of town-houses.

In Inch TD, just west of Balrothery, there are the low remains of a mound set on the top of a drumlin-like rise. It is situated on the opposite side of the main road to the church, which is also built upon a similar high point. Was the church also built on the site of an older monument?

The northernmost site in County Dublin is on the coast, 1.5km north of Balbriggan in **Bremore** TD. At Bremore, very close to the sea, there are five mounds, presumably passage tombs. The site has the classic form of relatively small monuments associated with a larger mound; a pattern seen at other passage tomb cemeteries across Ireland. The largest stands at 3m high and 25m in diameter. This group forms the start of a series of passage tombs that flank the River Delvin. On the high ground to the north and south of Naul there are two further groups of passage tombs at **Knockbrack** (see below) and one of the most important Irish passage tomb cemeteries at Fourknocks (Co. Meath). At the time of writing there is talk of building a new harbour very close to the Bremore complex, which would ruin a beautiful, almost perfect part of Ireland. One and a half kilometres north-west, just 400m over the Meath border, there is another passage tomb in Knocknagin TD, which probably belongs to this group.

The Monuments of the Dublin Plain

This discussion of the inland monuments of County Dublin starts with a fine barrow, at the north end, 4km west of Naul in **Westown North** TD. When viewed from the road it appears to be massive. It is quite large, but it has been cleverly sited on the top of a natural mound which enhances its appearance. It is in very good condition and appears to be relatively untouched. The mound has two tiers. The lower one is 20m in diameter and 1.5m high. The upper layer is 1.5m high, approximately 12m in diameter and centred on the lower level.

Either side of the boundary between **Kitchenstown** and **Knockbrack** TDs, 2km south-east of Naul, on a steep, north-facing slope above the River Delvin, there is a passage-tomb cemetery. Across the valley, in County Meath, is the renowned passage-tomb cemetery at Fourknocks.

The **Knockbrack** cemetery consists of five mounds. Hartnett first brought it to the attention of archaeologists in 1957, but it was not until 1983 that a proper description was made by David Keeling. The three most ruinous of these are in **Kitchenstown**, while the remaining two are in **Knockbrack**. The largest mound is 2m tall and 12.5m in diameter. On the summit of the hill, 500m south of the five mounds there is another mound, also in **Knockbrack** TD. The hilltop is also the site of a large hill fort that was only identified from aerial photographs.

The southern slopes of the hill are much gentler. On these there is a much denuded mound in **Hollywood Great** TD. The southerly views from here are unbroken until the Dublin Mountains. To the north the mound on the summit of **Knockbrack** dominates the skyline.

West of Hollywood Great there is a line of four mounds spread out over a distance of 11km. These are in Mallahow, Adamstown, Garristown and Newtown TDs. A continuation of this line extends to a mound in Primatestown TD across the Meath border and a pair of henges on Windmill Hill, also in County Meath. The Garristown and Adamstown mounds stood on prime farming land and have been ploughed away. From the site of the Garristown mound it is possible to look across the River Delvin to the far side of the valley where the Fourknocks

Knockbrack from the south

The Mourne Mountains from the site of the Garristown mound

passage-tomb cemetery stands. Beyond that the Mourne Mountains can be seen 75km north in County Down.

The Mallahow mound stands so close to the road that the roadside drainage ditch cuts through its north side. The mass of trees planted upon it make it difficult to fully appreciate, but it appears to be around 15m in diameter and 2m high.

In Skidoo TD, 2.5km south of Ballyboghil on the R108, another mound is marked on the Ordnance Survey maps, but it is located on a stud farm and strict quarantine procedures restrict access.

Three kilometres east of Ballyboghil, near to the old nunnery in Gracedieu TD, there is another mound marked on the Ordnance Survey map, but little can be seen of it today. There was another mound in Shallon TD that has now disappeared also.

In the grounds of Stewart's Hospital in **Palmerstown** TD there is a ring barrow. This occupies a ridge-top position that overlooks an early church site. The barrow is heavily planted, but on close inspection you can see its encircling ditch and bank just inside the treeline.

One and a half kilometres south-east there is a kist in **Knockmaree** TD, on Knockmary Hill, in Phoenix Park next to St Mary's Hospital. Its kidney-shaped capstone is broken into many pieces and has been badly cemented back together – some of the joints are breaking apart again. It is held just 20cm off the ground by three small stones and an additional concrete pillar. These inconspicuous remains are all that is left of a fine kist discovered by workmen whilst levelling a mound in 1838. As well as the kist, which contained three skeletons, there were also four Bronze Age cists inserted into the mound containing secondary burials. There is a reconstruction of the main kist on display inside the Phoenix Park Visitor Centre.

In March 2006 this monument got a mention in the Oireachtas:

> Aengus Ó Snodaigh asked the Minister for Finance the reason the Office of Public Works have failed to protect the cromlech at Knockmary Hill, Phoenix Park, Dublin 20, which has been deteriorating in recent years due to traffic and other activity; and when the plaque explaining the history of the cromlech will be erected by the Office of Public Works.

He also asked if there was any possibility that an archaeological dig could be carried out, as a survey in 1959 had identified a Bronze Age settlement in the vicinity. The response said that:

> An archaeological inspection carried out in 2003 at the portal tomb at Knockmary Hill, Phoenix Park, reported no evidence of damage at this monument since the capstone was repaired in 1973.

The minister went on to say that digs were only normally undertaken when a site was in danger, but the possibility of erecting a plaque would be investigated. The kist is actually some way off the road, so the first question seems a little odd. Furthermore, the mound was flattened in 1838, making any excavation here pointless. An information sign to this monument – or any monument for that matter – would be a welcome addition! Oh, and it is not a portal tomb. Who's advising the man responsible for the well-being of Ireland's heritage?

The trees to the immediate south of the kist obscure the view, but by moving to one side of them you can see that the Dublin/Wicklow Mountains are easily

The Dublin/Wicklow Mountains. From right to left: Seahan, Seefingan, Piperstown Hill (by the smoke between the treetops and the far mountains), Kipur with TV mast and Killakee at the left edge

visible from here. It is not until you stand at this point and look to the south that you realise how high up Phoenix Park is. This is one of the only sites in Dublin where you can clearly see the tombs at **Ticknock**, **Tibradden**, **Seahan**, **Montpelier**, **Slievthoul** and Seefingan (County Wicklow).

There is another kist, which was moved from **Chapelizod** TD, close to **Knockmaree**, and is now in the tapir enclosure at **Dublin Zoo**. This is of a completely different design to its former neighbour and much better preserved. The capstone is a more uniform shape and held aloft by two parallel slabs that form the walls of a chamber measuring around 80cm high, 40cm wide and 60cm deep. A fourth slab forms the floor of the chamber.

A mound in Drimnagh TD, close to Drimnagh Castle, was excavated in 1938, when the site came under threat from quarrying. Part of the site was even quarried away while the dig was in progress! What seemed to be an ordinary mound turned out to be hiding an extraordinary monument. The main mound covered an earlier mound, at the centre of which there was a small burial chamber containing a skeleton and a unique 'hanging-bowl'. Alongside this there was a fire pit and a stone-built chimney. The inner mound was covered in charred tree trunks. When the fire was lit the mound must have looked like a mini volcano at night, with a red glow or possibly even flames coming from the top. Secondary burials into the outer mound included a fine, upturned cinerary urn containing a cremation set onto the top of the inner mound, and a cremation accompanied by a food vessel.

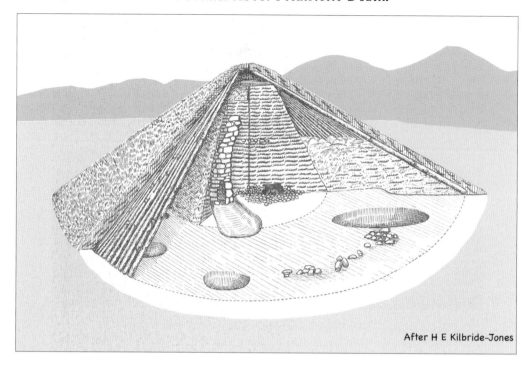

After H E Kilbride-Jones

In **Kingswood** TD, in Ballymount Park next to the Tallaght Luas line, just south of junction 9 on the M50, there is a 4m high, 20m diameter mound.

A Bronze Age cemetery was excavated in Edmonstown in 1951 and the remains of twenty-seven people were found buried in a mixture of pits and cists. A hole in one skull indicates that it may have been trepanned. One of the pits contained a decorated urn, which held the cremated remains of an adult, two children and an infant. The crouched skeleton of an adult occupied one of the cists. Pottery vessels were found in thirteen of the burials.

In the grounds of an old nunnery in **Leopardstown**, in an area that is now a playing field, there is a small standing stone. This is just 1m tall and is slightly tilted. It is set very close to a granite rock outcrop.

The final site to consider is on **Athgoe Hill**, 3km west of Rathcoole. There are several barrows on the hill, with the largest occupying the highest point of the hill. This barrow is very well defined by a circular bank and ditch. The depth of the ditch is up to 1m when measured from the top of the bank. There is a break in the bank on the north-east side, which appears to line up with Howth. The bank also shows signs of being faced with large stones, which means it may actually be a henge similar in design to the one at **Lugg** and not a barrow after all.

Athgoe Hill can be looked upon as the last foothill of the Dublin Mountains. It is clearly visible from many of the monuments that are spread across their north-western peaks, such as **Seahan**, **Slievethoul** and Lugmore. Likewise, you are

Right: Lepoardstown standing stone

Opposite: Reconstruction of
the mound at Drimnagh. *(After
Killbride-Jones)*

rewarded with stunning views towards the Dublin/Wicklow Mountains from the
main barrow/henge, and fine views over the Dublin and Kildare plane. From the
site of the main monument described above, the large passage tomb and cairn
on **Seahan** and the cairn on Seefingan (County Wicklow) are clearly visible,
whereas the passage tomb on Seefin (County Wicklow) is hidden behind Saggart
Hill. However, it is possible to know where the Seefin passage tomb is, because
the large cairn at the northern end of **Slievethoul** TD on Saggart Hill marks its
direction. If this alignment was deliberately engineered, then Athgoe Hill and its
possible henge take on a new level of importance in Dublin's prehistoric landscape.

Afterthought

Although there is some overlap, the Neolithic monuments of County Dublin can be divided into several groups. With the exception of **Howth Demesne**, the portal tombs are found across the foothills of the Dublin Mountains. They are all built between 30m and 250m above sea level and they are all within 500m of a stream. The four wedge tombs in the area are found in the same region as the portal tombs, but are built between 60m and 350m above sea level. Their similar design closely links them, making it quite likely that the same group of people constructed them all. The passage tombs have two ranges. There are the mountaintop sites along the Dublin Mountains and the band of monuments that line the coastal region.

Several of the monuments act as key focal points to many of the other sites. The **Fairy Castle** passage tomb at **Ticknock**, on Two Rocks Mountain, can be seen from most parts of the county and the masts on Three Rocks Mountain allow us to quickly locate them on the skyline. The aerials next to the monuments in **Slievethoul** TD on Saggart Hill, help us to identify their location easily, the obelisk on Dalkey Hill and the lead mine chimney on Carrickgollogan also act as good markers for getting your bearings. The whole of Howth is so clearly visible from any high point and with its almost recumbent 'sleeping beauty' profile, it must have been a special place in the minds of the prehistoric peoples of the Dublin area.

The early habitation of sites such as Feltrim Hill and Dalkey Island during the Mesolithic period, and the richness of later Neolithic, Bronze Age and Iron Age monuments in the Dublin area, show that this has always been an important region. If the great monuments of Newgrange, Knowth and Dowth had been built alongside the Liffey, then the obvious prehistoric importance of the county would have been popularised years ago and would today be common knowledge. As things stand the local heritage just gets in the way. Maintaining it is time-consuming and time is money. Once, landowners used to keep monuments clear, often because they respected the history associated with them. They knew the lore attached to the site and recognised their historic importance and may have been superstitious about damaging them. This attitude is now even fading outside of the big city and many wonderful monuments are being neglected. Nowadays, in many but not all cases, they are simply in the way.

The ever-growing nature of Dublin City is obstructing the views from many sites. It is this progress that is our heritage's greatest enemy today. If a site of national importance was discovered during preparation for an office development for a huge multinational company, it is hard to imagine that the preservation of the monument would be of prime concern. It would probably be excavated in a hurry, recorded and then destroyed so that the offices could be built. It seems that today, in the battle of history and heritage versus money there can only be one winner! This process also brings another problem: with so many sites being excavated in such a short space of time, the excavation reports do not get published. The commercial excavation companies are obviously there to make money and writing and publishing reports is not a great money-spinner.

There is no way to bring back the ploughed-out mounds and barrows, but there is still time to save the sites that remain. More of them must be taken into state care, so that their future can be secured.

Megalithic Monuments

'Megalithic' is one of those adjectives that does exactly what is says on the box. It is derived from two Greek words: 'mega' meaning large and 'líthos' meaning stone. Obviously, the term megalithic monument is a very broad one, which covers all types of prehistoric sites created through the use of large stones, and so, to make things easier, this broad classification has been broken down into sub-categories such as 'standing stones', 'stone circles', 'passage tombs' and so on (all of which will be discussed in further detail below). All of these different categories have their own defining features, some of which are incredibly obvious, some of which are quite subtle. With the exception of the barrows and some of the standing stones, the monuments in this book date from the period known as the Neolithic or New Stone Age. The beginning of the Neolithic period in Ireland was pushed back in time in the late 1990s from 3500 BCE to 5500 BCE with the use of radiocarbon dating on the tombs at Carrowmore in Sligo. It ended around 2000 BCE when the Bronze Age started.

For visiting ancient sites I recommend using the Ordnance Survey (OS) maps. When looking at an OS map you will see most of the historical sites marked by a red dot with an accompanying categorical title. The ones that concern this book are 'Artificial Mound', 'Barrow', 'Bullaun Stone', 'Cairn', 'Standing Stone(s)', 'Stone Circle', 'Stone Row' and 'Megalithic Tomb'. The addition of 'Bullaun Stone' to this list is my own. Bullaun stones are not generally accepted as being megalithic monuments, but I will argue their case later on. 'Megalithic Tomb' is a generic term, which covers many different types of sepulchral monuments:

court tombs, kists, passage tombs, portal tombs and wedge tombs. The differences between these types will also be described shortly. Most people know these types of monument by the terms cromlech or dolmen. The use of the word 'tomb' in these names has come into question, mainly because excavations are beginning to show that relatively sparse remains were interred within most of these monuments. The scarcity of human remains in many (but not all) of these monuments has been attributed to the acidic soil found in most parts of Ireland, which may be the case, but this lack of evidence is beginning to lead some to reconsider the role that the monuments played in the lives of the Ancients who built them. They are now being viewed more as a ritual building with a much broader purpose, perhaps closer to modern churches than some would like to believe.

Monument Types That Appear in This Book

Artificial Mounds

Across the country there are many man-made mounds that are not classified as barrows, mottes or passage tombs mainly because they have never been properly explored.

The vast majority of artificial mounds are round in plan and hemispherical in shape. These could be sod-covered cairns or simply piles of earth. Others, such as **Drumnigh**, are rectangular in plan with flat tops. Every one of them could be a burial monument, but some are likely to have been built as either viewing platforms or to mark the location of a long-forgotten event such as a battle.

Until each site is individually researched their purpose will never be certain. For instance, the **Drumnigh** mound, mentioned above, is north-west of Howth and Howth becomes visible when you stand on top of it. Was this rectangular platform constructed in order to allow the builders to witness the winter solstice sunrise over Howth? Only careful observation at the correct time of year will verify this.

Barrows

Although barrows are not Neolithic, and certainly not megalithic in most cases, they are included here because their location can tell us a lot about habitation areas in both the Neolithic and the period immediately following – the Bronze Age. In their most common form they consist of a raised earthen mound, which is often surrounded by a fosse (a ditch around a monument) and a bank.

Unfortunately, the fact that barrows tended to be built near to habitation sites has its negative side too, because it means that they are often located on good quality land. This has led to many of them being ploughed away, leaving them difficult to identify, especially from the ground. A great many potential sites are identified through crop marks in aerial photographs, a distinctive change in the appearance of a crop when viewed from the air, by the underlying monument altering soil conditions above it.

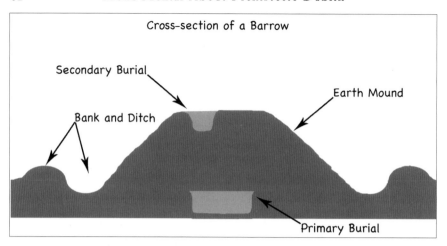

Cross-section of a barrow

The area covered by a barrow can vary from as little as 5m to over 30m in diameter, but the average is in the region of 10m. Due to erosion and damage caused by ploughing it is difficult to define a typical height for barrows, but some of the better-preserved large examples approach 3m in height.

Burial rite is usually a single inhumation or a cremated burial. The burials are generally centrally placed, either in a pit or in a stone- or wood-lined chamber called a cist, which may or may not be covered by a capstone or wooden lid. Later, secondary burials are often found inserted into the covering mound.

One interesting contrast between megalithic monuments and barrows is that barrows often occur in groups or barrow cemeteries. Of the megalithic monuments only passage tombs share this trait.

There are several distinctive designs of barrow. Bell or bowl barrows are the simplest type – a simple round mound. Some examples have a well-defined bank and ditch, usually referred to as a fosse, encircling them, whereas others have no fosse or bank. Long barrows are rare in Ireland and more common in England; they are elongated in plan with the burial(s) set towards one end. The earliest English examples, such as West Kennett, have megalithic chambers. Pond barrows are another rare style; they are indicated by a waterlogged depression surrounded by a bank and fosse and are not at all common in Ireland. Ring barrows are more like mini henges; they have no mound, but consist of a flat circular area demarked by a bank and fosse.

One very fine example of a ring barrow can be seen at *Belgade Deer Park*. This has a very well defined fosse and is clearly visible as it is at the roadside. One very nice bell barrow can be seen within the area covered by this book, on *Newtown Hill* to the rear of Johnny Fox's Pub, an area rich in monuments. Another good example is on Ballyremon Commons (Co. Wicklow) in the shadow of both the Great Sugar Loaf Mountain and Djouce.

Bullaun Stones

A bullaun is a large man-made depression in a stone. They can vary in size from 10cm to 40cm in diameter. Usually there are one or two bullauns in a stone, but multiple examples are not a rarity. The phrase 'bullaun stone' refers to the whole stone. The actual bullauns are usually hemispherical but can be conical or flat bottomed either. Occasionally a bullaun breaks the edge of the stone, which often seems to have been a deliberate design feature.

They are nearly always by water, usually running, but are often to be found by wells. They often appear in churchyards, either having been moved there to be used as a font or stoop or serving to indicate that the church occupies a much older sacred location. Both these reasons point to the ritual use of bullauns still being prominent when Christianity first came to Ireland. As part of the conversion to Christianity, their assimilation of the 'Celtic' populace must have been a major step in the process. This is also implied by the presence of bullaun stones at sites/shrines associated with St Brigit, the latter-day incarnation of Brigid, a Celtic goddess of fertility and life.

This assimilation may not have been the first. They are usually thought to date from the Late Bronze Age (shortened to LBA in academia) or the Iron Age. However, I think some examples date back to Neolithic times (e.g. **Glassamucky Mountain**) and their lasting association with the life-giving St Brigit/Brigid may date back a great deal further than is currently thought, perhaps to some older fertility goddess cult. Many are still used in religious rites at holy wells and the water that collects within the bullaun depressions is often said to cure things such as warts and headaches.

Most of Dublin's examples of bullaun stones are now associated with early religious sites, such as **Kil of the Grange** and **Rathmichael** churches. In addition, around Glendalough in County Wicklow there are thirty or more examples. These are focused around the monastic settlement there and along the old route now known as St Kevin's Way, a trail leading across the Wicklow Mountains from Hollywood on the west side to Glendalough on the east side. This trail, which follows an ancient roadway, speaks against the one theory that bullauns were originally instruments for grinding corn, unless it was for making a ritual gruel or similar meal which was eaten on pilgrimages along the route. Another concentration occurs in the Glen of Imail on the western side of the Wicklow Mountains.

I have not attempted to include all of the bullaun stones in the county, but have listed the ones I feel are prehistoric in origin.

Cists/Kists

A cist is a stone- or wood-lined burial chamber that is set into the ground, often covered by a wooden or stone lid. They are found beneath barrows and cairns, and can contain inhumations or cremations. They date from either the Bronze Age or Iron Age. Occasionally, they occur as secondary burials inserted into the cairns of earlier Neolithic monuments. The cairn of **Kilmashogue** wedge tomb has two good examples.

The word kist is used to describe small stone burial chambers that are built above ground, usually covered by a cairn. They are usually four-sided and have a large capstone. Kists are generally Neolithic in date and contain inhumations.

Archaeologists mainly use the word cist to describe both types, but it is easier to make the distinction by using kist for the more megalithic versions.

Henges

Although the word 'henge' was originally coined to describe the 'hanging stones' at Stonehenge in Wiltshire, England, the term is now used to categorise a very different monument. Henges are circular, earthen structures created by digging a ditch and raising a bank on the outside. It is common for there to be an entrance on the eastern side, formed by leaving a gap in the bank with a causeway across the internal ditch.

In the majority of cases very little archaeological evidence is uncovered within the enclosed area, leading to the conclusion that they were solely ritual monuments. When excavations do uncover evidence of activity it is often quite remarkable (see **Lugg**). Some monuments that are classed as henges have an external bank, which means that many of Ireland's raths or fortified homesteads could have started out as henges. Some of the larger ring barrows, such as the one on the top of **Athgoe Hill**, could also be henges.

Passage Tombs

Passage tombs are so called because the burial chamber is reached via a passage leading from the outer edge of the covering mound or cairn. The walls of the passage, like those of the chamber, are usually constructed from large slabs standing up on end known as orthostats, but can be of dry stone walling. The roof of the passage is constructed by placing large slabs on the tops of the orthostats. The chamber roof can be either made from similar horizontally laid slabs or by a process called corbelling. Corbelling is the process of placing successive layers of stones on top of each other, decreasing the gap with each layer to reduce the span until only a small opening remains. A single stone is placed across the space to form the last part of the roof. The chamber in Newgrange has one of the finest examples of a corbelled roof.

The internal chambers of passage tombs vary in design. The 'classic' style is the cruciform chamber, where the main chamber has three sub-chambers leading off it, one opposite the passage and one off either side, forming a cross when viewed from above. In others the chamber is little more than a slight widening of the passage. Such examples are called undifferentiated passage tombs. The famous tomb at Newgrange has one of the finest cruciform chambers and Ireland's largest example, Knowth, has both a cruciform and an undifferentiated chamber.

County Dublin contains only a few ruined passage tombs, the most conspicuous of which is on the summit of Two Rocks Mountain at **Ticknock** and is visible to thousands each day as they drive southbound on the M50, not that many of them notice it or realise what it is. All that can be seen now is the collapsed cairn, but reports from the 1800s say that locals told of a 'cave' on one side, indicating that it is/was a passage tomb. On **Montpellier**, a neighbouring hill now popularly known as the Hell Fire Club, there once stood two other examples, the material from which was used to build the hunting lodge, the ruins of which can be seen for miles around standing next to their original site. A few lumps and bumps on the hilltop behind the building are the only remaining traces of these two tombs. A standing stone from the hilltop was also incorporated into the building.

To the south there are several passage tombs on other peaks in the Wicklow Mountains, such as those occupying the top of **Seahan** in County Dublin, and Seefin and Seefingan (both in County Wicklow). This trio of mountains inspires thoughts of the triple goddess, especially those on Seefin and Seahan when viewed from around Brittas, where they look like nipples on huge breasts. Surely this was not by coincidence.

In north County Dublin, along the coast, lie several passage tombs, the first of which used to lie to the north of Rush, but is sadly now ruined beyond definite identification. Past Skerries there are or were examples at **Knockbrack**, Knockan, Hampton Demesne, Knocknagin and a passage-tomb cemetery stands on the coast at **Bremore**. All except the **Bremore** and **Knockbrack** complexes are ruinous. Inland from these sites stands a very important ridge with many monuments upon it and it is not the Boyne Valley, but Fourknocks, where one of the finest and most unusual passage tombs stands.

Except for the coastal examples passage tombs occupy the highest locations of all the tomb types. Two of the possible reasons for this are that the builders either wanted to stamp their presence on the landscape by building monuments that are visible for miles around or that there was a desire to create the monuments as close to the heavens as possible to be nearer their gods. The real reason may be far more complex and incorporate both these ideas.

Nationally passage tombs occupy positions in the north-west, north and east of the country, with one exception in County Cork and the recently discovered group at Ballycarty just outside Tralee in County Kerry. At one time it was believed that they had their origins in the fine examples found in the Boyne Valley and that they deteriorated in design and quality as the people who built them migrated west. However, it is now known that the passage-tomb cemetery at Carrowmore in County Sligo is home to the oldest scientifically-dated megalithic monuments in Europe. In County Waterford there are several examples of undifferentiated passage tombs at Carriglong, Matthewstown and Harristown, which are related to similar monuments found on the Isles of Scilly.

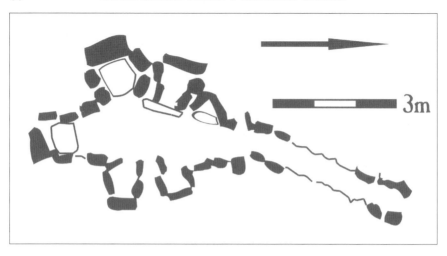

Above: Plan of the passage tomb on Seefin, County Wicklow. *(After Herity)*

Opposite: Stylised side view of a typical portal tomb. *(After Mongey)*

Portal Tombs

Whereas passage tombs often occupy the most dramatic locations, portal tombs are, more often than not, situated in more subtle places such as in valleys or at the base of hills. This does not mean, however, that they are not spectacular in their own right, because the general characteristics of the class make them the most visually striking of all the tombs. These are the monuments that are usually referred to as dolmens or cromlechs.

Portal tombs are often grouped together with wedge and court tombs in the larger group of 'gallery tombs', but the chambers of portal tombs are never sub-divided by jambs or sill stones. A sill stone is a low stone set across the width of an opening and a jamb is a tall stone set against the wall of the chamber opposite another, leaving a space between them.

Whilst the many similarities between the different styles must be considered, this is, in the author's opinion, enough to warrant portal tombs being placed in a class of their own. The main argument is that the portal stones derive from the entrance jambs of court tombs and a small number of portal tombs show some signs of having a degenerate court such as can be seen at Ahaglaslin (Co. Cork).

The single chamber is usually formed with just three walls: a single slab forms the rear (the backstone) and in most cases single stones form the two sides of this box-like construction. Set in front of each of the sides is a taller stone, which projects forward occasionally inline with them, but they are more usually set just outside the side stones. Together these form an entrance or a 'portal' and are referred to as portal stones. Between these there is often an inset door stone,

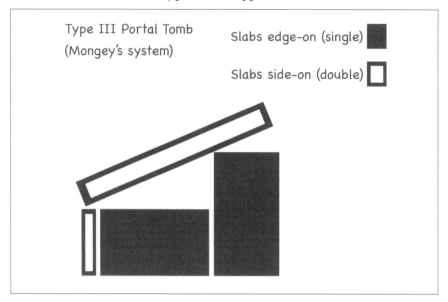

Type III Portal Tomb
(Mongey's system)

Slabs edge-on (single)

Slabs side-on (double)

which occupies the full width of the portal and forms an alcove. The height of these door stones varies and can be half-, three-quarter- or full-height.

The structure is finished off with the capstone, a huge slab or block of stone that forms a roof. One end of this rests on the backstone with the other end resting on the portal stones. The front of the capstone projects forwards beyond the portal stones, creating a very dramatic and imposing monument when viewed in profile.

It does not seem to be the case that portal tombs were necessarily incorporated in a mound or cairn, but in many cases evidence of some form of cairn survives. In such cases the monument is placed towards or at one end of a long sub-rectangular cairn. In no surviving instance does the cairn cover the capstone and many believe that portal tombs were never intended to be entirely covered. Given their visually imposing form, this is more than likely. It would appear that the capstones were meant to be left exposed and that the cairn, when present, only served to hide the outside of the chamber walls.

County Dublin actually has one of the highest concentrations of portal tombs in Ireland, a fact that surprises most people. When the area is extended to include north Wicklow the number of examples becomes even more impressive. Of these, the diminutive tomb at **Ballybrack** is the most publicly accessible. The finest examples in the area, and indeed two of the finest in the country, are at **Kiltiernan Domain** and **Brennanstown**, both of which are on private land, but can usually be visited on request. At least two portal tombs in the immediate vicinity of Dublin, one of them quite splendid in appearance in Shankhill TD (see above), have been destroyed.

Portal tombs have a wide distribution that is broadly similar to that of the passage tombs, but with two examples in County Cork.

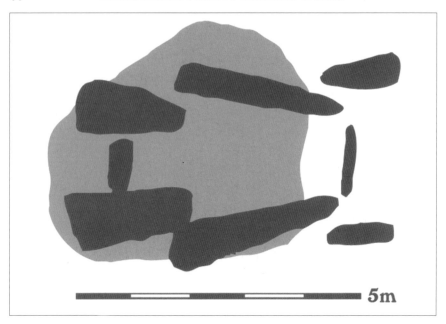

Plan of Brennanstown portal tomb. *(After Evans)*

Rock Art

There are two main types of rock art to be found in Ireland: that found decorating flat panels of bedrock or individual standing stones, and the more famous passage tomb art found decorating places such as Newgrange. When I refer to a site as being rock art I am using the term in the first sense: as carved panels or stones.

The motifs used on this type of carving are fairly consistent although some 'oddball' sites exist. The most common designs are cup marks – a small round depression – and concentric circles. There is only one known example of a spiral carved on a rock panel in Ireland (Rathgeran in County Carlow).

Armed with these two simple elements people have created some fantastic designs. By combining the two, the cup and ring motif is created. Sometimes a gutter is added, which emanates from the central cup mark and cuts through the surrounding rings. The Rathgeran stone mentioned above has two such designs placed side by side, with the gutter connecting the two central cup marks.

Other forms include the rare ladder motif and the cup mark with concentric penannular rings: rings that are broken.

The national distribution of rock art is unknown due to the likelihood that so many lie undiscovered below peat deposits. There are large concentrations around the copper-yielding areas of counties Cork and Kerry as well as in County Donegal. County Louth lost several good groups of panels through field clearance in the late 1900s and many others have been allowed to become overgrown to protect them. The combination of unrecorded loss through destruction and landowners allowing panels to be covered up, makes visiting rock art a difficult task.

Vast quantities of rock art are being discovered in the UK through the concentrated efforts of amateur rock-art hunters. There is no reason why, with the same sort of dedication, new rock art could not still be found in Ireland.

There are only two accepted examples of rock art in County Dublin: the southern face of the standing stone at **Raheen** has a large group of cup marks and a stone in the cairn at **Ballyedmonduff** is decorated with a small cluster of cup marks. There are several other possible rock-art sites within the county mentioned below. The nearest 'proper' rock art is in north Wicklow.

Standing Stones

What name could be more descriptive? Also known as menhirs or monoliths, standing stones are the simplest form, structurally, of megalithic monument and the most common. They are quite simply stones that have been stood up intentionally by man, with one end set into the ground. However, their original purpose is far from straightforward for they have been erected during many time periods and for many different reasons.

Some were originally boundary markers, others such as the huge Punchestown standing stone (Co. Kildare) were erected to mark burials, while others marked locations significant to the Ancients and, just to add to the confusion, many were erected in modern times as scratching posts for cattle. Sometimes standing stones are found in association with stone circles. These are known as outliers.

Despite having such a basic form (what can be more basic than a single stone?) standing stones come in a massive variety of shapes and sizes and are the most varied of the monuments. At one extreme you have giant, phallic examples such as the Punchestown or Forenaghts Great standing stones (both in County Kildare) and at the other extreme you have small, stumpy ones such as Knockiernan Lower (Co. Wicklow). Regardless of a stone's size or shape it is often possible to identify why that particular stone was selected. The **Glencullen** standing stone, for instance, is a beautiful cuboid block of solid quartz. Quartz plays a smaller, less obvious role in many standing stones that have thin bands or veins of quartz running through them creating the impression of a flesh and blood, living rock with pulsating veins.

Stone Circles

Stone circles are just that, stones arranged in a circle, but again it is not that simple; there are many styles of stone circles. In Scotland for instance there are the Recumbent Stone Circles (RSCs) that have a massive altar-like horizontal stone set between two towering flanking stones. In County Cork there are the Axial Stone Circles that have an odd number of stones, usually 5, 7, 11 or 19, where the odd stone is low and broad and the other stones then increase in height as they

Looking past the Piperstown standing stone along the Glenasmole Valley

progress away from this, the axial stone. In County Derry there are stone circles that are made of short stones and often have a tangential stone row of similar stature. Although these localised trends exist, the types are not limited to these areas. This is due to either a migration of ideas or of people, but more study is needed before this can be determined.

Stone circles are the most popular of all the megalithic monuments. It is easy to put this down to the publicity that the spectacular solar event at Stonehenge in England has received. Alternatively it is easier to imagine what a ruined stone circle may have once looked like, compared with the effort required to conjure up an accurate image of a ruined tomb in its youth. But stone circles deserve far more merit than this.

The almost total lack of knowledge regarding the original purpose of stone circles, or the manner in which they were utilised, allows everyone to speculate and retain their own fantasy. Several have been found to contain burials, but this does not make them burial monuments. It is more likely that these burials were sacrificial offerings to the gods of the builders, just as it used to be common practice to enclose a live cat during the construction of houses to ward off evil spirits.

Many purposes have been proposed and in some instances proven. For example, the stone circles at Grange Lios (Co. Limerick) and Drombeg (Co. Cork) have confirmed solstice alignments. Proof that a particular sample had key alignment features does not necessarily mean that they all did. It is this element of the mysterious, coupled with the fascination with the long forgotten knowledge of the Ancients, which helps to make stone circles so popular. The circle is also the simplest shape to produce and associate with and throughout history it has been used to symbolise the cycle and eternal nature of life and death.

Stone circles are scarce along the east coast of Ireland, but County Dublin and County Wicklow have several examples each in their mountainous areas.

Stone Rows & Stone Pairs

When standing stones are grouped together in a straight line, they become a stone row or an alignment. Two parallel stone rows form an avenue. Stone rows can be very short with just two stones or much longer – up to seven stones is quite common in Ireland. Some have even more. As with single standing stones, the shape and size of the stones forming a row can vary greatly, even within a particular stone row. In Cork, for example, it is common for the stones to rise in height from one end to the other.

Occasionally the stones that occur in pairs are separated from the main group of stone rows and referred to as stone pairs. These can often be interpreted as being a male/female pairing because one stone is more slender and phallic in appearance than the other, which is usually more blunt and rounded.

Dublin has several alignments: stone pairs in **Boherboy** and **Newtown Hill** TDs, a three-stone row in **Cunard** TD and the remains of a row in **Kilmashogue** TD.

Wedge Tombs

Wedge tombs have a sub-rectangular gallery divided into sub-chambers by low, full-width stones called sill stones or by two full-height stones set opposite each other known as jambs, leaving a narrow gap in between. This latter form is less common and shows a connection with court tombs.

They are called wedge tombs because of their distinctive shape. The front of the monument, which generally faces in a westerly direction, is both wider and taller than its rear.

A single stone spanning the entire width usually blocks the entrance. Two apparently localised trends differ from this rule. The wedge tombs of County Clare tend to have two stones blocking the entrance and those in Northern Ireland often have a single narrow stone centrally placed, which splits the entrance into two halves.

Some have a sealed off sub-chamber built onto the rear of the gallery (see **Ballyedmonduff**). Other more common architectural features also occur, called antechambers and porticos. These are both constructs attached to the front of the gallery, which are basically external sub-chambers. The main difference is that porticos are not closed at the front and are sometimes split in two by a vertical orthostat set along the central axis of the gallery.

'Adam and Eve' at Boherboy

The majority of wedge tombs were originally incorporated into a mound or cairn. The more simple structures were usually set into the centre of a round cairn, whereas the monuments with porticos etc. were often built into a D-shaped mound with the front of the gallery occupying a central position on the flat face. These D-shaped mounds can be quite exaggerated, giving more of a U-shape. It is quite common for the mound to have a small kerb. In a few rare instances more than one gallery was incorporated into a single mound. When this does occur the galleries are always parallel to one another and have their entrances facing in the same direction.

Another question that must be addressed concerns the true role of these structures in the society of their builders. Their portrayal as communal burial places is contradicted by the lack of remains found in the few examples to have been investigated to date. Wedge tombs were built with sealed galleries, whereas the majority of court tombs, portal tombs and passage tombs are constructed to make them more accessible. This would indicate that wedge tombs were final resting places, but perhaps the other types were built as 'mortuary houses', where remains were only placed inside for a short period of time before being removed for disposal elsewhere, at a yearly ceremony for instance. This would certainly help explain the apparent lack of remains found at some sites.

Wedge tombs are by far the most numerous of the 'sepulchral' monuments in Ireland and, unlike all the other megalithic tombs, have a nationwide distribution. They are nearly always located with an eye to the surrounding views, usually to the west, but they rarely occupy the highest point in an area.

Gazetteer Introduction

The gazetteer is organised alphabetically by townland, which to some might be a little confusing as some of these sites are known by other names such as the Glendruid dolmen in **Brennanstown**. I have chosen to use townlands as the primary index because this is how Irish monuments are catalogued in the archaeological inventories. If this practice was more widely used, then cross-referencing sites would be far easier between resources. Where they exist, the common names for monuments are listed in the indexes and mentioned in the text.

The author has visited all the sites included, but it should be borne in mind that most of these sites, although under state protection, are on private property and permission to visit should always be sought, unless they are clearly sign-posted.

Not every type of prehistoric monument that exists in Ireland is represented in the area surrounding Dublin, the most notable absence being court tombs, which do not occur en masse in the south, although there are a couple of instances in central south Ireland, several in Clare and one in Tipperary. Fortunately, County Dublin is blessed with magnificent passage tombs, portal tombs, standing stones, stone circles and wedge tombs.

Accompanying each description is the information needed to find it. For most, directions will be given from the nearest town or landmark, the exceptions being where the directions are simply crazy due to the amount of small roads involved. These directions will get you to the monument, but their presence here does not necessarily mean that there is a right of way. All of the entries will have the grid reference and the Ordnance Survey map on which it can be found. Except for the major places it is recommend that the Ordnance Survey maps are used when planning journeys, but a small word of warning – at the time of writing the road system of Ireland is undergoing so many alterations that often maps are out of date. For best results try to obtain the 3rd edition (or later if available) maps from the *Discovery Series*. These are available from all good bookstores and from the National Map Centre in Dublin, or directly from the Ordnance Survey of Ireland.

If, through this work, just a handful of people are given the inspiration to go out on a Sunday and become acquainted with some of Ireland's heritage, beyond tourist traps such as Newgrange, then it will have been worthwhile. This is not to demean the importance of Newgrange, but to say that it should be seen as just the beginning and not the end of one's journey into learning about the wondrous monuments left to us by Ireland's early inhabitants.

Notes About Visiting Sites

Most of the monuments in this book are on private land and, no matter how you feel about property being theft and all that, you must respect this when visiting a site. Any damage or nuisance you cause could jeopardise the chances of other people being able to visit.

Always get permission to visit a site if necessary.

When on farmland take care not to disturb livestock or damage crops.

Leave gates as you find them. If they are shut, shut them after you have passed through. If they are open, leave them open.

Always use paths where available and always walk around the edge of fields.

Never leave litter behind. THIS INCLUDES TEALIGHTS, CANDLES AND 'OFFERINGS' TO YOUR GODS OF CHOICE. People who visit after you do not want to be confronted with rotting flowers and wax-covered stones. Hot wax, along with being unsightly, kills the lichen that has taken many, many years to grow.

Take any litter you come across away with you and dispose of it properly. I have returned from some trips with a black bag full of other people's rubbish.

Do not light fires in or near to monuments, you risk destroying unexcavated evidence just below the surface and the resultant black burnt patches are very unsightly for those who follow after.

Do not remove anything (except for litter) from a site.

Do not chalk-in rock art to make it clearer. Take a bottle of water and pour it over the carvings. The reflections will make it just as clear as chalk does and no damage is caused to the stones.

Have a thought for others who may be present. You might enjoy loud music while at the stones, but those around you may not.

Enjoy yourself.

One rule sums up all of the above (and more) very nicely:

LEAVE ONLY FOOTPRINTS
AND
TAKE ONLY MEMORIES

Alphabetical Index

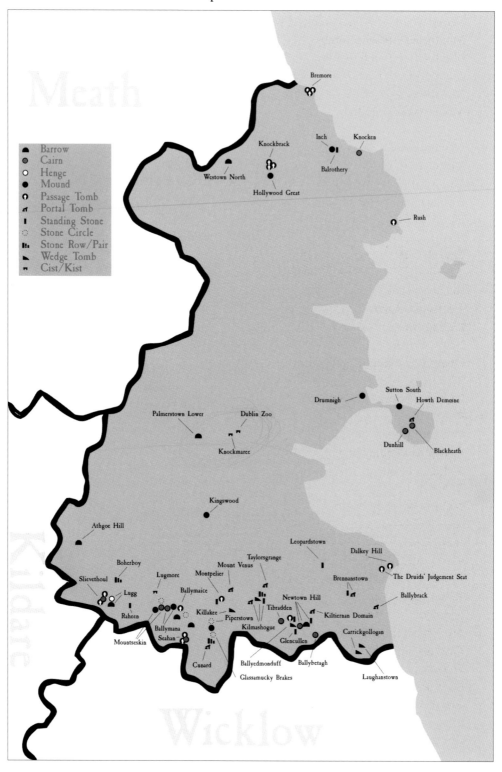

Meath

Kildare

Wicklow

Barrow
Cairn
Henge
Mound
Passage Tomb
Portal Tomb
Standing Stone
Stone Circle
Stone Row/Pair
Wedge Tomb
Cist/Kist

Bremore

Knockbrack

Inch   Knocken

Westown North   Balrothery

Hollywood Great

Rush

Drumnigh   Sutton South
                Howth Demesne

Palmerstown Lower   Dublin Zoo

Knockmaree   Dunhill   Blackheath

Kingswood

Athgoe Hill

Leopardstown   Dalkey Hill

Boherboy   Taylorsgrange
                Mount Venus   The Druids' Judgement Seat
Slievethoul   Lugmore   Montpelier
                                        Brennanstown
                Ballymaice
        Lugg   Ballybrack
                        Newtown Hill
Raheen   Killakee   Tibradden
                        Piperstown   Kiltiernan Domain
Ballymana   Kilmashogue
Mountseskin   Seahan   Carrickgollogan
                        Glencullen
                Cunard   Ballyedmonduff   Ballybetagh
                        Glassamucky Brakes   Laughanstown

Monument Type Index

Portal Tombs

Standing Stones

Stone Circles

Stone Rows/Pairs

Wedge Tombs

Monuments by
Council Area

Dublin City
Chapelizod – kist (see Dublin Zoological Gardens)
Dublin Zoological Gardens – kist
Knockmaree – kist
Palmerstown Lower – barrow
Stewart's Hospital – barrow (see Palmerstown)

Dun Laoghaire & Rathdown
Ballybetagh – cairn
Ballybrack – portal tomb
Ballyedmonduff – wedge tomb
Brennanstown – portal tomb
Brennanstown – standing stone
Cabinteely – portal tomb (see Brennanstown)
Carrickgollogan – wedge tomb
Dalkey Hill – passage tomb
Druids' Judgment Seat, The – passage tomb (see Killiney)
Fairy Castle – passage tomb (see Ticknock)
Glencullen – standing stone
Glendruid – portal tomb (see Brennanstown)
Kill of the Grange – bullaun stone
Killiney – passage tomb
Kilmashogue – portal tomb
Kilmashogue – standing stone
Kilmashogue – stone pair
Kilmashogue – wedge tomb
Kiltiernan Domain – portal tomb
Laughanstown – wedge tomb
Leopardstown – standing stone

Newtown Hill – barrow
Newtown Hill – cairn
Newtown Hill – hut site/ring cairn
Newtown Hill – standing stone
Newtown Hill – stone row
Oissin's Grave – cairn (see Newtown Hill)
Queen Mab – standing stone (see Glencullen)
Taylorsgrange – portal tomb
Tibradden – chambered cairn
Ticknock – passage tomb
Ticknock – standing stone
Two Rocks Mountain – passage tomb (see Ticknock)

Fingal
Balrothery – standing stone
Blackheath – chambered cairn
Bremore – passage tombs
Drumnigh – mound
Dunhill – cairn
Hollywood Great – mound
Howth – cairn (see Dunhill & Blackheath)
Howth Demesne – portal tomb
Knockbrack/Kitchenstown – passage tombs
Knocken – cairn
Knocklea – passage tomb (see Rush)
Rush – passage tomb
Sutton South – mound

South Dublin
Adam and Eve – stone pair (see Boherboy)
Athgoe Hill – barrow
Ballinascorney Upper – barrow
Ballymaice – passage tomb
Ballymana – cairn
Ballymana – mound
Ballymana – stone circle
Belgard Deer Park – barrow
Belgard Deer Park – stone circle
Boherboy – stone pair
Crockaunadreenagh – passage tomb
Crookan Cairn – cairn (see Ballymana)
Cunard – portal tomb

Cunard – stone row

Glassamucky – mound

Glassamucky Brakes – stone circle

Glassamucky Mountain – bullaun stone

Hell Fire Club – passage tombs (see Montpelier)

Killakee – wedge tomb

Kingswood – mound

Knockanavea – cairn (see Mountseskin)

Knockandinny – cairn (see Slievethoul)

Knockanteedan – mound (see Glassamucky)

Knockanvinidee – mound (see Ballymana)

Lugg – barrow cemetery

Lugg – henge

Macey Woods – wedge tomb (see Killakee)

Montpelier – passage tombs

Montpelier – standing stone

Mount Venus – portal tomb

Mountseskin – cairn

Mountseskin – mound

Piperstown – standing stone

Piperstown – stone circle and settlement

Raheen – standing stone

Seahan 1 – passage tomb

Seahan 2 – cairn

Seahan 3 – passage tomb

Seahan 4 – passage tomb

Slievethoul – cairn

Slievethoul 1 – passage tomb

Slievethoul 2 – passage tomb

Athgoe Hill
Barrows
OS Sheet 50: O 992 273

Directions: *Head west from Newcastle and take the left-hand turn just after the old church. After 500m take the left fork and continue for a little over 1km to the first road on the right. Park near to this junction. Walk back towards Newcastle and look out for an orange and yellow barrier across a track on the right-hand side of the road. Walk up this track to the top of the hill where you will see the banks of the barrow in the field to your right.*

The main barrow is on the very highest point of the hill in the shadow of the microwave aerial mast. The central area is 20m in diameter and defined by an

The two main monuments on Seahan seen from Athgoe Hill

encircling ditch with an external bank. The height of the bank is now around 1m from the base of the ditch, but was probably much higher originally, the bank having been reduced by ploughing and the 1.5m wide ditch having silted up somewhat.

There is a break in the bank on the north-eastern side, which, repeating a familiar pattern, would appear to be aligned towards Howth. There are indications that the faces of the bank and ditch are lined with stone, in a similar fashion to the henge at *Lugg*, which, along with the entrance through the external bank, could indicate that this is actually a henge and not a barrow.

The view to the east is dominated by the Dublin/Wicklow Mountains, in particular Saggart Hill, with *Seahan* and Seefingan (County Wicklow) standing proud above it. Seefin (County Wicklow) is conspicuously hidden behind Saggart Hill, but the cairn at the northern end of *Slievethoul* TD on Saggart Hill marks its position.

Mini-Gazetteer: 1.5km E there is a barrow on Lyons Hill (Co. Kildare). 3.1km SE there is a passage tomb at *Crockaunadreenagh*. 6km SW there is a henge and standing stone at Forenaghts Great (Co. Kildare). 9km ENE there is a mound at *Kingswood*.

Looking towards Ballymana from Ballynascorney Upper

Ballinascorney Upper
Barrow
OS Sheet 50: O 081 221

Directions: *An Ordnance Survey map is not required in order to reach this site. It is best to approach via the forest track that leads towards the site from the south. When you reach the end of this track continue through the woods down to the boundary wall and walk along the far side of it to reach the site.*

Not a great deal remains of this barrow now and it is almost impossible to spot on the ground. At first the choice of location, which is in the saddle between Slievenabawnoge and Carrigeenoura hills, seems odd, but after looking around for a while I began to appreciate the site.

For those interested in the interrelationship between sites this is a very good location to visit. From here the sites of the monuments on Saggart Hill are visible, although trees on the hill prevent you seeing them directly. The aerials above the Slievethoul monuments are a useful guide. To the east the **Fairy Castle** passage tomb in **Ticknock** TD can be seen on Two Rocks Mountain along with the tors on Three Rocks Mountain. The pine plantation to the south prevents you from seeing in that direction, but the view to the north is only partially blocked by Slievenabawnoge.

The most interesting alignment to another monument is that which lies past the western edge of Slievenabawnoge and is connected to **Knockanividee** mound in Ballymana.

Mini-Gazetteer: 900m NW there is a barrow at **Belgard Deer Park**. 3.5km NW there is a cist at Lugmore. 5.9km S there is a fine passage tomb on Seefin Hill (Co. Wicklow). 8km SW at Ballward (Co. Wicklow) there is a stone circle.

Ballybetagh
Cairn
OS Sheet 50: O 203 203

Directions: *This cairn is not easily accessible as it is alongside a private driveway.*

This cairn is one of several mounds recorded in Ballybetagh during the 1837 report for the Ordnance Survey. All but this one seem to have now disappeared. As seen from the road it is quite substantial, reaching a height of several metres and 25m in diameter.

Other monuments recorded in the area included stone circles, which may have been the kerbs of cairns stolen from elsewhere.

Ballybetagh Bog is of exceptional importance to early Irish prehistory due to the large quantities of *Megaceros giganteus* or Giant Irish Deer skeletons that have been recovered from it. You have to wonder what prehistoric people would have made of the skulls and antlers of these great beasts if they had dug them up.

Mini-Gazetteer: 1.2km W there is a standing stone at ***Glencullen***. 2.9km SSE there is a kist at Parknasilog (Co. Wicklow). 5km S there is a portal tomb at Onagh/Glaskenny (Co. Wicklow). 8km S there is a barrow at Ballyremon Commons (Co. Wicklow).

Ballybrack
Portal Tomb
OS Sheet 50: O 255 233

Directions: *Follow the N11 south from Dublin to the Shankhill roundabout. Turn left towards Shankhill. At the first roundabout turn left onto Shanganagh Road. Continue to the next roundabout where you will see the tomb to the left in front of you just past the entrance to the Cromlech Fields Housing Estate.*

Ballybrack portal tomb is a really interesting monument, not only due to it being a very small example of its genre (a size which is only really matched by **Cunard**, also in County Dublin), but because it is a miracle that it is still standing at all. Its diminutive size almost makes it a boulder burial, a status only really denied to it by the height of its supporting stones.

The capstone stands on four stones in all, arranged in two evenly matched pairs. If two of these stones are the portal stones then the chamber is, unusually, just formed from two stones – the shorter two of the four to the west. It is unlikely to have ever had a door stone.

There is no visible sign of a cairn, but this is hardly surprising. In fact, it is far more surprising that anything of this monument remains at all considering its location. Until the mid-twentieth century it stood in a farmer's field, but it now

Ballybrack portal tomb from the south

Ballybrack in 1851

Ballybrack in 1851

stands in the centre of a communal green, at the front of the Cromlech Fields Housing Estate. It has somehow escaped the road-building process and nearly managed to escape the rigours of modern life. There are, unfortunately, traces of red spray paint to be seen on the capstone, added no doubt, by some angst-ridden teenagers with nothing better to do – a sad reflection upon our times.

The tomb is composed of local Wicklow granite and is aligned east to west, with portal stones located facing the east. The underside of the capstone shows considerable wear, probably having been formed from a split boulder and then flattened.

A very nice little stone plaque stands a few metres from the tomb proclaiming it to date back to 2500 BC, which is a pretty good estimate, although it could be up to 750 years older. P.J. Hartnett found a flint knife within 3m of the tomb (date of find unknown).

Mini-Gazetteer: 2.1km W there is a wedge tomb at *Laughanstown*. 5.8km W there is a portal tomb at *Kiltiernan Domain*. 6.3km NW there is a standing stone at *Leopardstown*. 9.4km S there is a standing stone at Kilmurry (Co. Wicklow).

Ballyedmonduff
Wedge Tomb
OS Sheet 50: O 185 213

Directions: *The easiest place to start out from in order to reach this site is Glencullen – follow the signs for Johnny Fox's Pub. From the pub head north for 1km, passing the golf course, until you reach a gate on the left. Through here lies a path that leads straight across the field to another gate that takes you into the pine trees. Take this path and once in the trees, follow it around to the left. After about 500m, when the trees open up and you are walking next to the golf course, the path turns sharply right. The tomb is visible in the trees just 50m after this bend.*

Drawings of this tomb dating from the nineteenth century show a very different picture of this monument to the one that welcomes the visitor today. Photographs taken at the time of the 1940s excavation works, show an entirely different picture again. At the time of excavation, the tomb was almost indistinguishable from the surrounding heather-covered ground. Although the restoration work brought many interesting features to light, it has to be said that the tomb may have suffered slightly because of it.

The kerb that retains the cairn material is U-shaped with the base of the U, at the rear of the tomb, facing east. The gallery is over 6m long and features double walling. It is partitioned by a septal slab, creating a separate chamber at its east end. The stone forming the back wall of this chamber has a fine horizontal band of quartzite running through it; an obvious reason for its selection.

Ballyedmonduff wedge tomb – looking over the gallery from the south-west

The kerbstones on the south side of Ballymaice passage tomb

At the front of the gallery are traces of an ante and some of the façade stones are also present, although some of these look out of place.

The greatest drawback of this site has to be the fact that it is now embedded in a pine plantation and the wonderful views that it once offered towards the Great Sugar Loaf Mountain, have been obscured. It is impossible not to reach the conclusion that this view was a primary consideration when the location was first chosen and, because the tomb is close to the edge of the plantation, it would not be very difficult to restore this view for visitors to enjoy once more. Hopefully, with the growing appreciation of the landscape and its relationship with monuments, this can one day be achieved.

The photographs taken at the time of excavation mentioned above, also show that the two tors that give Two Rocks Mountain its name were clearly visible from this site and appeared to be set along the skyline. Today the pine trees block this spectacle as well.

The excavations uncovered some Beaker pottery allowing the tomb to be dated to around 2100 BCE.

Mini-Gazetteer: 1.7km NW there is a passage tomb known as the **Fairy Castle** at **Ticknock** on Two Rocks Mountain. 3.8km WNW there is a chambered cairn at **Tibradden**. 5.4km E there is a bullaun stone at **Rathmichael**. 6.4km SSE there is some rock art in Onagh (Co. Wicklow).

Ballymaice
Passage Tomb
OS Sheet 50: O 070 236

Directions: *From Brittas follow the signs for Bohernabreena along the R114. After 2km the road veers to a sharp left. Continue for a further 2km and take the second road on the left. This single-lane road rises and turns sharply. Continue until you reach a parking area near to some bungalows. Park here and walk along the track through the trees. After 150m there is a firebreak on the right. Walk along this and head for the Scotch pine trees, where you will find the tomb.*

The group of large Scotch pine trees that tower above these remains make the tomb quite easy to locate. About three quarters of the 10m diameter kerb remain in place, mainly on the south side. Several large stones that can be seen lying a few yards away were presumably taken from the kerb at some time. In the centre of the monument a rectangular arrangement of stones appears to be the remains of the chamber.

This is the easternmost site in a large complex of monuments spread across Tallaght Hill, all of which offer superb views across the city of Dublin and seem especially placed to view Howth.

Mini-Gazetteer: 1.6km NW there is a cist & barrow at Lugmore. 4.5km E there are passage tombs on Hell Fire Club Hill at **Montpelier**. 7.2km WSW are two standing stones in Tinode (Co. Wicklow). 9.9km south there is a barrow at Ballynabrocky (Co. Wicklow).

Ballymana
Crookan Cairn
Cairn
OS Sheet 50: O 065 239

Directions: *From Brittas follow the signs for Bohernabreena along the R114. After 2km the road turns sharply left. Continue for a further 2km and take the second road on*

Looking past Crookan Cairn towards Howth. A portion of the kerb can be seen to the right

the left. This single-lane road rises and turns sharply. Continue until you reach a parking area near to some bungalows. Park here and walk along the track through the trees. The main group of monuments on Tallaght Hill, of which this is one, lie in the fields on the far side of the trees to the right of the track. To reach them pick a suitable route through the trees to the fence at the top. You should see the main mound from here. Crookan Cairn is next to this mound.

This is part of the complex network of sites on Tallaght Hill. The cairn is unusually oval in plan and surrounded by a kerb of large, unmatched boulders. Standing at the east end of the mound in an altar-like fashion there is an interesting stone that seems to be of great significance. It is a large boulder that has been split just above a diagonal quartz seam, so that its upper face has a thin layer of quartz covering it. This sloping surface faces outwards towards Howth and the Lugnasadh sunrise.

The cairn is adjacent to the large mound on the hilltop and so quite easy to find, but beware of the many ponds that surround them.

Observations of significant solar alignments have been made from the top of Tallaght Hill and it may be that this cairn holds the key to them.

Mini-Gazetteer: 2.7k W there is a standing stone at **Raheen**. 4.4km SSE there is a cairn and passage tomb on **Seahan Hill**. 6.6km SW there are two standing stones at Tinode (Co. Wicklow). 9.5km E there is The Brehon's Chair portal tomb at **Taylorsgrange**.

Looking over Knockanvinidee towards Howth

Ballymana
Knockanvinidee
Artificial Mound
OS Sheet 50: O 065 235

Directions: *From Brittas follow the signs for Bohernabreena along the R114. After 2km the road turns sharply left. Continue for a further 2km and take the second road on the left. This single-lane road rises and turns sharply. Continue until you reach a parking area near to some bungalows. Park here and walk along the track through the trees. The main group of monuments on Tallaght Hill, of which this is one, lie in the fields on the far side of the trees to the right of the track. To reach them pick a suitable route through the trees to the fence at the top. You should see the mound from here.*

This huge mound is the centrepiece of the Tallaght Hill complex. It is 4m high and has a maximum diameter of 40m. When viewed from the west its profile seems to match that of Howth, which is visible over the top of it. This is probably coincidental though and due to disturbance by mound robbers.

Of the many monuments on the hill the mound called Knockanvinidee is the largest, but Crookan Cairn immediately to the west is the most interesting. The site is surrounded by dew ponds that may have been enhanced.

It has been suggested that this mound was actually built as a viewing platform to watch the sun rise above Howth around the festival of Lugnasadh in August, when the gathering of the harvest used to be celebrated at many hilltop sites, including Tallaght Hill. The large, sloping kerbstone at Crookan Cairn, a few metres away (see previous entry), also indicates the possible importance of this alignment.

One of the small stones of Ballymana stone circle with two more beyond

Mini-Gazetteer: 500m ENE there is a passage tomb at **Ballymaice**. 3.3km NW there is a stone pair called Adam and Eve at **Boherboy**. 4.3km SSW there is a cairn at Ballyfolan (Co. Wicklow). 9.8km S there is a barrow at Ballynabrocky (Co. Wicklow).

Ballymana
Stone Circle
OS Sheet 50: O 064 239

Directions: *From Brittas follow the signs for Bohernabreena along the R114. After 2km the road turns sharply left. Continue for a further 2km and take the second road on the left. This single-lane road rises and turns sharply. Continue until you reach a parking area near to some bungalows. Park here and walk along the track through the trees. The main group of monuments on Tallaght Hill, of which this is one, is in the fields on the far side of the trees to the right of the track. To reach them pick a suitable route through the trees to the fence at the top. You should see the main mound from here. Beyond the mound there is a cattle crush and beyond that a new plantation. The stone circle is between this plantation and the raised bank that separates the fields from the trees, 100m from the crush.*

A little over 100m from Crookan Cairn, between a field wall and newly planted pine saplings are four evenly spaced low stones. These may be the remains of one of the stone circles reported on the hilltop in the 1800s.

Balrothery standing stone in somewhat uncomfortable surroundings

All four of the stones are set into the ground and are evenly spaced, suggesting they were once part of a stone circle. The tallest stone is just 70cm high. Another similar stone stands 30m to the east and may be an outlier.

Mini-Gazetteer: 1.7km W there is a mound at **Mountseskin**. 4.5km W there is a passage tomb at **Slievethoul** on Saggart Hill. 6km E there is a wedge tomb at **Killakee**. 12.7km SSW there is a passage tomb at Lugnagun (Co. Wicklow).

Balrothery
Standing Stone
OS Sheet 43: O 202 612

Directions: *From the N1/M1 take the R132 north into Balrothery. At the crossroads turn right and the take the second left. After 150m you should see a new housing estate on your right. The stone is at the far end of the central green.*

The surroundings of this standing stone have really changed in the last few years. Until recently it stood on a low rise in a boggy field on the western edge of the village. It now forms the centrepiece to a new housing development that completely surrounds it.

The stone is 1.6m tall and roughly 60cm square in plan with a bulge on one side.

Mini-Gazetteer: 4.9km WSW there is a passage-tomb cemetery at **Knockbrack**. 5.8km SW there is a mound at **Hollywood Great**. 9km WNW there is a mound at Herbertstown (Co. Meath). 10.1km W there is a henge at Heathtown (Co. Meath).

Belgard Deer Park
Barrow
OS Sheet 50: O 073 226

Directions: *From Brittas follow the signs for Bohernabreena along the R114. After 2km the road turns sharply left. Continue for a further 2km and take the second road on the left. This single-lane road rises and turns sharply. The barrow is situated in the field to the left of the road immediately after this bend.*

As with most ring barrows there is very little to see here, but it is a very good example of its type. It is quite easy to make out the 20m diameter ditch and bank that surround the flat central area. The site's positioning at the head of the road from Bohernabreena makes this an important landmark and if there were a raised mound at its centre it would have been a very imposing site for people travelling through the pass.

Mini-Gazetteer: 900m ESE there is a barrow at **Ballinascorney Upper**. 2.6km NNW there is a cist at Lugmore. 3.8km SW there is a cairn at Ballyfolan (Co. Wicklow). 5.1km E there is a wedge tomb at **Killakee**.

Belgard Deer Park
Stone Circle
OS Sheet 50: O 075 234

Directions: *From Brittas follow the signs for Bohernabreena along the R114. After 2km the road turns sharply left. Continue for a further 2km and take the second road on the left. This single-lane road rises and turns sharply. As you drive up this road you will reach some pine trees on the right-hand side of the road. The stone circle is 150m across two fields, from the gate next to these trees.*

Not much of this monument remains due to the farming activity on these fertile slopes. An arc of stones is all that is left on the north side. Some of them are loose and could either be general field clearance or displaced stones from the other side of the stone circle.

Mini-Gazetteer: 3.7km W there is a standing stone at **Raheen**. 4km E there is a passage tomb at **Montpelier** on Hell Fire Club Hill. 7.2km E there is a portal tomb at **Kilmashogue**. 9.4km S there is a standing stone at Athdown (Co. Wicklow)

The remaining stones of Belgard Deer Park circle

Blackheath
Chambered Cairn
OS Sheet 50: O 280 379

Directions: *Drive to Howth via the R105 from Dublin. You will reach a crossroads where the R106 continues north. Turn right here and head south around the island. After passing a cemetery on the right and the entrance to the golf course on the left you will come to a left turn. Take this road and follow it around until shortly after a sharp right bend. You should see a track leading over the hill to the left. Park here and follow this track. Keep heading north-west around the top, keeping the golf course on your left and heading towards Ireland's Eye. The cairn is on the far north-western corner.*

Most of the cairn material has been stolen away leaving a thin spread of rubble across an area 10m in diameter. At the centre of this is a stone-lined cist where the burial would have been placed. This central chamber is too small to have held a crouched burial, leading to the conclusion that it held a cremation.

Of all the monuments found on Howth the two remaining cairns (see **Dunhill** for the other) offer the best views that take in Ireland's Eye and Lambay Island to the north and the Dublin and Wicklow Mountains to the south-west. When viewed from here the two islands line up so that Lambay sits above Ireland's Eye and perhaps this alignment was the reason for choosing this location. The site also looks down on Muck Rock, on the far side of which is the portal tomb in **Howth Demesne**.

The small cist at Blackheath

Mini-Gazetteer: 500m NW there is a portal tomb at **Howth Demesne**. 2.2km NW there is a mound at **Sutton South**. 6.4km NW there is a mound at **Drumnigh**. 13.3km SW there is a standing stone at **Leopardstown**.

Boherboy
Adam and Eve
Stone Pair
OS Sheet 50: O 043 259

Directions: *Take the N81 west from Tallaght. 300m after the N82 turn-off, the main road bears left, while a road carries on to Saggart. Take this turn and drive for 1km where you will come to a left-hand turn. The stones are in the field on the left just after this lane.*

Across Ireland there are many stone pairs, but these are the only examples that fall within the area covered by this book. Luckily, they rank amongst the finest and are very easy to visit.

As can be seen in the photograph the two stones have different shapes: the more westerly stone being very square, while the other is more pointed. This is quite a standard feature of stones pairs and it is this difference that has led to these particular stones being called 'Adam and Eve' locally. This gives them roots in ancient fertility rites as it suggests that they have a long-standing history of being differentiated by gender.

Boherboy stone pair with Saggart Hill in the background

More often than not it is the more pointed stone that is associated with the male aspect, presumably a phallic reference, while the squarer stone represents the female. Unusually, despite having a groove in the top, it is the squarer stone of these two that is called Adam – perhaps making reference to the broad shoulders of a man, rather than to sexual organs. As with so many things, this 'perversion' of the norm could be a late change brought about by a little Christian prudence.

Mini-Gazetteer: 1.9km SE there is a cist at Lugmore. 6.1km S there is a ring cairn at Ballyfolan (Co. Wicklow). 7km SSW there are two standing stones at Tinode (Co. Wicklow). 9.5km SE there is a portal tomb at **Cunard**.

Bremore
Passage-Tomb Cemetery
OS Sheet 43: O 197 660

Directions: *Head north from Balbriggan along the coast road (R132). About 500m after leaving the town take a right-hand turn down an unmarked farm track. Park near to the barns and continue along the track on foot till you reach its end. The mounds are arranged right on the cliff edge 300m north-east of the end of the track.*

This is the largest remaining group of a series of mounds and passage tombs that stretch along Dublin's east coast from Rush to Laytown. Of the five mounds marked on the Ordnance Survey map only four are easy to make out, the fifth is

Bremore viewed from the beach to the north

just discernable as an almost-ploughed-away bump in the centre of the field to the east of the main mound.

The largest mound is 3m high and 15m across. The tide is slowly eroding the rocky shore next to the main group and the three smaller mounds are in danger of collapsing into the sea. These are all also overgrown with gorse. This complex stands near to the estuary of the River Delvin, which winds its way inland past Naul. Many mounds and passage tomb cemeteries, including those at **Kitchenstown/Knockbrack** and Fourknocks just over the county border in Meath, flank the river's route. Like the Boyne to the north, which receives far more attention due to the three amazing tombs at Newgrange, Knowth and Dowth, the River Delvin must have once been an important river to the passage tomb builders.

Just offshore are the Cardy Rocks, a group of small rocky outcrops that disappear at high tide. To the south south-east, 7km off the mainland, lies Rockabill, which is easy to spot by its lighthouse. Further investigation is needed to see if there are any significant sunrise alignments over Rockabill from Bremore, perhaps around the vernal equinox.

Mini-Gazetteer: 1.5km WNW there is a passage tomb at Knocknagin (Co. Meath). 4.8km S there is standing stone at **Balrothery**. 9.7km WSW there is a passage tomb at Fourknocks (Co. Meath). 13.3km NNW there is a stone row at Baltray (Co. Meath).

Brennanstown portal tomb from the north

Brennanstown
Glendruid
Portal Tomb
OS Sheet 50: O 229 242

Directions: *From the N11 take the Cabinteely exit. After 800m you will go around a sharp right bend. On the right you will see a driveway in which you can park. Access to the tomb is via Dolmen House opposite. Please ask. Another way to access the site is via the old railway line at the rear of Brennanstown Vale: from Brennanstown Road turn into Brennanstown Vale. Follow the road around until you reach a turning circle in the road. Park in this area. Just past the turning place there is a small trackway that leads to a gate. Walk down here and turn left after the gate – this is the disused railway line. Walk along the well-worn footpath until it crosses a bridge. Shortly after the bridge take the path that leads up over a wall and loops back under the bridge and brings you to the riverbank. Carry on in the same direction for a few hundred metres. Eventually you will see that the trees on both banks open up and the capstone of the tomb should be visible on the far bank. Ford the river with great care here and you are at the tomb.*

Also known as Cabinteely or, more popularly, 'Glendruid' dolmen, this tomb is one of the few portal tombs to be excavated in County Dublin. During this process it was also rebuilt, utilizing a concrete arch to help hold up the massive 30 ton capstone. This reinforcement is actually undertaken in a very discreet manner, as it is only visible from the inside.

The location of this monument is simply beautiful. It lies in a small valley to the rear of some private houses, but is almost hidden from them in a grove of mature trees. When standing next to it, it is extremely easy to forget that you are in sub-

Brennanstown portal tomb in 1851

urban Dublin. Walking down to it can be quite magical too, because this is one of the few portal tombs that you are able to approach from above.

Like **Kiltiernan Domain** the capstone is wedge-shaped in profile, which gives it the characteristic 20 degree slope. Although the chamber looks low from the outside it is possible to stand up within it, because the floor level inside is nearly 1m below the surrounding ground level. The 1.8m deep capstone seems to have been shaped to a blunt point and is supported by two well-matched portal stones, each weighing around 7 tons. Two large slabs lying recumbent form the 3.0m long and 1.8m wide chamber. The door stone is full height.

An unusual feature can be seen here at the rear of the tomb. Two arcs of stones, not much wider than the chamber, reach out as if forming a small court. A few portal tombs have traces of a forecourt, but this rear court is somewhat unique.

On the upper surface of the capstone is a man-made channel that seems to be there to divert any water that might flow down and into the small court at the rear. This sort of water management was found on the roof stones above the passage at Newgrange, County Meath, and is a very unusual feature. A wonderful urban myth exists regarding this channel, i.e. that is was there to divert blood when the Druids made sacrifices on the capstone, which of course is utter nonsense and is just typical of the late eighteenth-century obsession with Druids.

Mini-Gazetteer: 1.4km SSE there is a wedge tomb at **Laughlanstown**. 3.4km ENE there is a passage tomb on **Dalkey Hill**. 5km SW there is a cairn on **Newtown Hill**. 7.5km W there is a wedge tomb at **Kilmashogue**.

Brennanstown standing stone, taken from the old railway track to the south

Brennanstown
Standing Stone
OS Sheet 50: O 227 250

Directions: *It is not possible to access this stone.*

   The stone is situated in a field overlooking Glendruid and its portal tomb, but large trees obscure them from each other. Despite being in a built-up area, this standing stone is extremely difficult to find and can be best seen from the old railway line that runs behind the Brennanstown Vale estate. It was moved 150m to its present location in 1993 to make way for a new housing development at the request of the developer. Luckily, prior to moving the stone, an excavation of the immediate surrounding area was undertaken and two pieces of burnt bone were discovered immediately in front of the stone, thus confirming its antiquity. This was not enough to fully protect it from being moved and in a minor battle of money versus heritage, money won.

Mini-Gazetteer: 3km NW there is a standing stone at **Leopardstown**. 5.6km SW there is a wedge tomb at **Ballyedmonduff**. 8.3km WSW there is a cairn at **Tibradden**. 8.6km W there is a standing stone at **Kilmashogue**.

Carrickgollogan
Wedge Tomb
OS Sheet 56: O 235 198

Directions: *Take the R117 from Dublin to Enniskerry. When you come to a Texaco petrol station bear left and take the first left. After about 1.5km you will reach a farm on the*

Carrickgollogan wedge tomb hiding in a hedgerow

left. Take the road/track beside this and follow it up the hill to the T-junction. Turn right and after about 200m you will pass a white house. The tomb is situated on the edge of their garden, overlooking the next field.

The first time I tried to find this tomb I failed. I managed to find the right field – the overhead power lines are a dead giveaway – but it was dusk and I did not really know what to expect here. My second visit was more fruitful though and I found the remains hiding in the hedgerow on the west side of the field. Three stones now stand forming a trilithon-type arrangement. I had hoped to find more of the structure in the hedgerow behind it, but this seems to be all that is left. The scant remains have made different people come to opposing conclusions about the nature of the tomb – was it a wedge tomb or a portal tomb?

This lonely ruin is all that remains of what was a whole host of cairns and tombs that apparently once stood all over Carrickgollogan Mountain. These were recorded in the Ordnance Survey letters in the early 1800s. It would appear that many of these structures were used in the construction of the lead mine chimney on the north side of the hill.

Mini-Gazetteer: 3km SW there is a kist at Parknasilog (Co. Wicklow). 4km NNE there is a portal tomb at *Ballybrack*. 6.5km S there is a cairn at Glencap Commons (Co. Wicklow). 10.9km SSW there is a passage tomb at Glasnamullen (Co. Wicklow).

The remaining orthostats of Crockaunadreenagh passage tomb

Crockaunadreenagh
Passage Tomb
Sheet 50: O 019 237

Directions: *The easiest way to reach this site is from the car park on Saggart Hill at grid reference O 024 235. From there walk up the track and continue over the first 'crossroads'. Continue until you reach a path on the right that runs alongside a fence. Take this path. After it crosses a gravel track make sure you are on the left-hand side of the fence. This path turns sharp left and takes you onto the top of the Knockananiller cairn. Crockaunadreenagh passage tomb is in the adjacent field and can be seen from the top of the cairn.*

Although in a different townland to Knockananiller cairn (see **Slievethoul**), this monument is just 20m from it and must be seen as part of the same complex. Just as at Knowth and Newgrange (both County Meath), where there are smaller orbital tombs around the main monument, this small passage tomb is associated with the larger cairn.

Unlike Knockananiller, this site has been disturbed and much of the cairn has been robbed away, leaving a handful of the passage orthostats exposed, the tallest of which is about 1m high. The passage aligns with the passage tomb in **Slievethoul** TD on the west side of Saggart Hill. The views to the north, from east to west, are extensive making this a great place to watch summer sunrises and sunsets over Dublin.

Crockaunadreenagh means the Little Hill of the Blackthorns, but whether this refers to the now lost barrow in the townland or to the passage tomb is not clear.

Mini-Gazetteer: 900m S there is a passage tomb at **Slievethoul**. 5.1km E there is a passage tomb at **Ballymaice**. 9.2km SE there is a passage tomb at Seefin (Co. Wicklow). 9.9km ESE there is a standing stone at **Piperstown**.

Cunard
Portal Tomb
OS Sheet 56: O 117 199

Directions: *From Ballyboden follow the Military Road (R115) south for 8km. Just before you cross the Wicklow border take a right turn (second right after the Killakee car park). A further 450m after a sharp right bend, you will cross a stream. Park here and walk down along the stream for 400m to the tomb.*

This little portal tomb does not make an appearance on the Ordnance Survey maps and therefore is hardly visited at all, because people are simply not aware of it. Situated out of sight on the slopes of a boggy hillside, 400m from the nearest road, casual passers-by are unlikely to stumble across it. This is possibly due to walkers being put off this area because of the inconsiderate people who ride trials bikes at the top of the slopes near the road, filling the air with a terrible din. This is unfortunate for several reasons, but primarily because this valley is, in my opinion, one of the most important early Neolithic centres of activity in County Dublin.

Cunard portal tomb (upper left) and the waterfall below it

The tomb itself is beautifully located on a small, slightly raised platform next to where two streams meet, circle its base, and then continue on to flow into the River Dodder below. To sit here, when there are no motorbikes interrupting the peace and tranquillity, is a great way to pass the time and gather your thoughts. The air is filled with the sounds of the stream dancing down its rocky path, and one can relax quite easily.

Immediately below the site there is a small waterfall. Where this has cut through the rock it is possible to see that the rocky outcrop the tomb stands on is not of the same rock as that which surrounds it. The rock beneath the tomb appears to be red with rust-like deposits, so perhaps this is an iron-rich deposit. Was this the reason for choosing this location?

The whole hillside around here is strewn with rocks and boulders of all sizes and so it is surprising that only such a small tomb was built, but I suppose it must have suited the needs of the people who constructed it.

It is aligned roughly north-west to south-east. The small, 2 ton capstone is a delightful kite shape when viewed from above, and rests on two stones which form a small chamber at the broader end. The more pointed end rests on the ground and it is difficult to say if two, now missing, portal stones once raised this end up.

There are several other arrangements of stones on these slopes, all alongside the stream, that could either be the remnants of similar structures or fortuitous formations. It is possible that this tomb was built by simply laying a capstone on top of two naturally placed rocks.

Mini-Gazetteer: 1.4km N there is a standing stone at **Piperstown**. 5.7km SW there is a passage tomb on **Seefin Hill**. 8.5km ENE there is a portal tomb at **Kiltiernan Domain**. 9km WSW there is a stone circle at Ballyfoyle (Co. Wicklow).

Cunard
Stone Row
OS Sheet 56: O 119 199

Directions: *From Ballyboden follow the Military Road (R115) south for 8km. Just before you cross the Wicklow border take a right turn (second right after the Killakee car park). A further 450m after a sharp right bend you will cross a stream. Park here and walk down along the stream for 200m to the find the stone row.*

This stone row consists of three pointed stones positioned amongst a mass of prostrate boulders. Like the nearby portal tomb (see previous entry) it too stands beside one of the larger streams that feed the River Dodder.

The stones are spaced at approximately 10m intervals running south-west to north-east along the slopes of the valley. The lower, southwest stone stands by

Left: The tallest stone in the Cunard stone row

Below: The obelisk on Dalkey Hill on the ancient mound

a level, circular platform-like area 8m in diameter, which could be part of the monument. This may have been a viewing platform of some kind. It would be interesting to know if the outcrop of rock that this platform is on, is of a similar rock type to that which the portal tomb below is built upon. The north-east stone has a notch in the top that seems to echo a notch on the horizon.

Mini-Gazetteer: 200m W there is a portal tomb also in *Cunard* TD. 3.4km N there is a wedge tomb at *Killakee*. 5.8km E there is a standing stone at *Kilmashogue*. 7.2km E there is a standing stone at *Glencullen*.

Dalkey Hill
Passage Tomb
OS Sheet 50: O 260 255

Directions: *Park at the public car park on the west side of the hill. Walk along the path away from the entrance and turn left to walk along the valley towards the coast. Just after a pair of gateposts the path divides to continue up each hill. Take the path up the steps to the right and walk to the top.*

The obelisk on the southern summit of Dalkey Hill stands on a very conspicuous grass-covered mound. Large stones can be seen in a few bare patches, indicating that the mound is quite likely to be a cairn. Given its hilltop position it is probably a passage tomb.

The whole of the hilltop is littered with rocky outcrops, some of which have interesting natural basins. The views to the south along the seafront to Bray Head are fantastic. To the north Howth seems to sit on top of the northern peak.

Hopefully, when restoration work begins on the obelisk, some time and resources will be made available to investigate the mound below it.

Mini-Gazetteer: 2.3km SW there is a portal tomb at *Ballybrack*. 5.8km WNW there is a standing stone at *Leopardstown*. 7.7km SW there is a cairn at *Ballybetagh*. 11.7km S there is a standing stone at Kilmurry (Co. Wicklow).

Drumnigh
Artificial Mound
OS Sheet 50: O 233 423

Directions: *From Portmarnock follow the R106 south towards Baldoyle and Howth. Just over Portmarnock Bridge the road turns sharply left and a side road continues off to the right. Take this side road. After 300m you will find the mound in a field to the right.*

This monument is really hard to get a handle on when you first see it. Unlike

The Drumnigh mound from the north-west

The kist from Chapelizod; now in the tapir enclosure at Dublin Zoo

all the other mounds in the area, which are round, this one is rectangular in plan. This makes it closer to the type of mound that would have covered some wedge tombs, rather than a possible passage tomb. However, once on the mound's flat top, its most likely purpose becomes evident.

The view from ground level in this field is very limited, but from the top of the mound you can suddenly see Howth to the south-east. Was this artificial mound created to provide a place from which to witness the winter solstice sunrise over Howth? There are no hills in this direction from which to watch this event.

The mound is 30m long, 15m wide and 3m high. At the south-east end it appears to have been quarried away or perhaps somebody attempted an excavation here to determine if it was perhaps a wedge tomb.

Mini-Gazetteer: 5.9km SE there is a portal tomb at **Howth Demesne**. 6.5km SW there is a cairn at **Dunhill**. 14.8km WSW there is a kist at **Knockmaree**. 15.6km S there is a standing stone at **Leopardstown**.

Dublin Zoological Gardens
Kist
OS Sheet 50: O 129 352

Directions: *This relocated monument is in the tapir and Patagonian mara enclosure at Dublin Zoo. It is difficult to see, though, as it is behind the tapirs' house and the ice cream shop.*

Well, you certainly don't expect to be surrounded by tapirs and Patagonian maras when you visit an ancient site. It must be quite unique in that respect. In spite of its small size, it is a very interesting monument. Two upright slabs of mudstone hold a thick, chunky block of mudstone 1m off the ground. In between the two standing upright, a fourth slab forms a floor to the small chamber.

The tomb was moved here from Chapelizod, probably from the vicinity of Phoenix Park where there is a kist (see **Knockmaree**).

Mini-Gazetteer: 2.4km WSW there is a kist at **Knockmaree**. 4.1km W there is a barrow at **Palmerstown Lower**. 10.1km SSE there is a portal tomb at **Taylorsgrange**. 10.9km SSE there is a wedge tomb at **Kilmashogue**.

Dunhill
Cairn
OS Sheet 50: O 284 373

Directions: *Dunhill can be approached from two directions. One is via a footpath leading from the cliff-top walk. The second leads from the other direction by taking a path across the golf course from the back of Muck Rock. For this route, follow the directions to Blackheath (above). From there carefully descend into the valley to the north. Follow the valley west to the edge of the golf course. Cross with care, following the white marker stones that mark the right of way. Once on the far side of the course the path goes up the hill to the cairn.*

The rounded peak of Dunhill is the highest point on Howth and so it is hardly surprising to find the remains of an ancient cairn on its summit. Only three kerbstones remain in place, but masses of the cairn material have been utilised close by to build walkers' shelters.

The three remaining kerbstones at Dunhill

The three stones are arranged around the western edge of a raised rocky out-crop, which has some scatters of small stones on it that may have been from the cairn. Nearby, as on much of the higher parts of Howth, the rock is riddled with quartz veins.

Mini-Gazetteer: 500m NE there is a cairn at **Blackheath**. 700m N there is a portal tomb at **Howth Demesne**. 6.4km NW there is a mound at **Drumnigh**.

Glassamucky
Knockanteedan
Mound
OS Sheet 50: O 091 231

Directions: *The nicest way to reach this mound is also one of the most difficult ways. This route is not for the faint-hearted. Walk along the reservoirs in Glenasmole and cross the lower dam to the steep wooded hillside. It is uphill from here and it is very, very steep. Like all ground beneath trees it can be mulchy and slippery underfoot, so take great care. Good walking boots are essential. At a height of 30m or so above the end of the dam, there is a pseudo style – a break in the barbed wire on top of the fence. Cross the fence and keep climbing upwards. At the top there is a large break in the hedgerow. Pass through this and then climb to the top of the field to another style. The mound is 20m into the field beyond the style.*

Seeming to guard the northern entrance to the Glenasmole Valley, at the top of a steep rise above the lower reservoir, this mound is a sad reflection of what it once must have been. Much of the top of this 15m diameter mound has been removed, leaving a large gouge in the top that runs out through its south side. It is now just 1.5m high. The west side, where the hedgerow lies nearest, is covered in gorse bushes.

Knockanteedan from the east

Knockanteedan translates to 'the little hill of the blasts or gusts', but it would be almost impossible to experience gusts here now, because of the high hedges that surround the mound. The same hedges also make it impossible to assess the original viewshed.

Mini-Gazetteer: 1.4km SW there is a barrow at **Ballinascorney Upper**. 2.5km ENE there is a standing stone and two passage tombs at **Montpelier**. 5.9km E there is a cairn at **Tibradden**. 9km SW there is a stone circle at Ballyfoyle (Co. Wicklow).

Glassamucky Brakes
Stone Circle
OS Sheet 50: O 115 209

Directions: *Take the R115 south from Rockbrook and after about 4km you will pass a turnoff to the right. Keep going past the parking area on the left. As you round a bend you will see a memorial 100m in front of you to the left. Just past this memorial is a left turn. Turn here and continue along this road until you pass another left turn. Park shortly after this junction and you will see a 'cattle crossing' sign in front of you. Walk 30m along the road beyond this and head directly up the hill. The circle is about a 50m climb.*

Nestled on the west-facing slopes above the River Dodder this little semi-ruined stone circle is actually the best-preserved example in Dublin and I think the only one that can definitely lay claim to its title. The stones on the eastern side, if any ever existed, are buried beneath earth and debris that has slipped down the hillside above. However, it could be that the circle was only ever complete on the downslope side. It is an axial stone circle, with the low, 1m long axial stone facing

Looking north-west over the axial stone of Glassamucky Brakes stone circle

north-west to watch the winter solstice sun sink over the top of Knockanvinidee, possibly one of the most important hills in Dublin's early history.

There are just seven stones still standing, forming an arc on the north-west corner, with a few fallen stones lying to the south-west. The centre of the circle forms a small plateau, 8m in diameter, on the hillside, almost certainly artificially constructed for the purpose. Somewhere on the hillside, amongst the countless boulders, there is said to be another stone circle, but I have never been able to identify it.

Across the valley and down below there are many signs of ancient habitation. At the roadside, directly below the circle, is a hut site and on the hillside opposite, old field systems can be observed.

Mini-Gazetteer: 1km SSE there is a portal tomb at **Cunard**. 2.7km N there is a standing stone and two passage tombs at **Montpelier**. 3.6km WSW there is a cairn and passage-tomb cemetery at **Seahan**. 7km E there is a wedge tomb at **Ballyedmonduff**.

Glassamucky Mountain
Bullaun Stone
OS Sheet 50: O 129 204

Directions: *Take the R115 south from Rockbrook and after about 4km you will pass a turnoff to the right. Keep going past the parking area on the left. As you round a bend you will see a memorial 100m in front of you to the left. There is a parking/pull-in space on this bend. Park here. You will see a track leading up the hill 15m behind you. Walk along this track for 120m or so and you will reach this great big stone.*

Looking over the Glassamucky Mountain bullaun stone towards the Great Sugar Loaf Mountain

What is a bullaun stone doing in a megalithic guidebook? Well, I believe that this stone really does warrant close inspection and perhaps that it even challenges conventional wisdom about bullaun stones. It may be necessary for us to reconsider the origins and ages of bullauns because of this stone. I am certain that it is a Neolithic and not a Bronze Age monument. What's more it has a very special property, one that, to my knowledge, has not been observed at any other bullaun stone, but more of that later.

The stone is 2m long, a little over 1m broad and stands 1.2m high. There is a single large bullaun, measuring over 30cm in diameter and 10cm deep, set in the centre of the top face. At the east end there are two more of similar sizes, but these are incomplete. It sits alongside an ancient pathway that leads over Glassamucky Mountain and is aligned north-east to south-west along its length.

The important aspect of this stone that I alluded to earlier is that it has definite solar alignment. Looking south you see the gentle slope of the hillside fall away to the west. Set exactly south-east, just poking over the false horizon created by the hillside, is the very tip of the Great Sugarloaf Mountain, marking the winter solstice sunrise in a no-nonsense manner. On the morning of the winter solstice the sun rises at the point marked by the peak and then proceeds along the top of Kippure Mountain.

Unlike most bullauns this one is not associated with any water feature that can be seen today, unless of course the ancient pathway was once a stream bed that disappeared with the appearance of peat. Dotted around the hillside are several features that may or may not be signs of habitation or ritual enclosures. An earthfast boulder stands 5m to the south of this stone. It is sub-cubic in form and has a line of elongated cup marks, evenly spaced in a straight line that also points straight towards the tip of the Great Sugarloaf.

Mini-Gazetteer: 2.7km NW there is a cairn at ***Piperstown***. 3.8km NNE there is a portal tomb in the grounds of Larch Hill Scout Camp at ***Kilmashogue***. 6.2km E there is a standing stone at ***Glencullen***. 8.5km SE there is a portal tomb at ***Onagh*** (Co. Wicklow).

Glencullen
Queen Mab
Standing Stone
OS Sheet 50: O 191 203

Directions: *From the N11 take the R116 through Kiltiernan and on to Glencullen. At Johnny Fox's Pub turn left. This stone is situated just over a low wall on the left about 150 yards after the junction.*

This square-sectioned, 1.6m tall stone is one of Ireland's most outstanding examples of a standing stone. It is a solid quartz monolith, measuring 1.1m along each side. The south face, which seems to have been deliberately flattened, positively glows in the midday sun, bringing home why the Irish for quartz is 'graincloch', meaning the sunstone. There is a stone in County Derry, in Cregg townland,

'Queen Mab' from the south west

which is a smaller version of this one. Apart from this stone I have only ever seen one other lump of solid quartz of this proportion and that was in a stream bed.

The people who erected this must have been delighted and amazed to find such a powerful-looking stone. It is hard to imagine that this was a solitary stone; its grandness really does call out for a more impressive setting, perhaps as the centrepiece of a stone circle. It is said that there was once another quartz standing stone in the area, which was known as The Stone of the Hound, but this was removed a long time ago and no record remains as to its new location. The name of this other monolith is hardly surprising as Glencullen means The Valley of the Hound.

There is one folk tale told about this stone, of a similar nature to tales attached to stones in many countries. It is said that a wealthy landowner once took a fancy to this stone and paid some locals to dig it up and move it to his front garden. However, when they attempted to do this, they dug down 20ft without finding its bottom and so gave up.

Mini-Gazetteer: 700m N there is a barrow, a cairn and a standing stone at *Newtown Hill*. 2.8km NW there is a passage tomb at *Ticknock*. 5km ENE there is a wedge tomb at *Laughanstown*. 7km NW there is a stone row at *Kilmashogue*.

Hollywood Great
Artificial Mound
OS Sheet 43: O 154 579

Directions: *Head north from Ballyboghil towards Naul on the R108 for 4km and then turn right at the crossroads. Continue for 800m or so and turn left. The mound is in the field to the left, opposite a factory a few hundred metres along this road.*

A lone thorn tree stands on top of this much denuded mound. The monument itself is nothing special, but its location is wonderful. High above to the north, the passage tomb on the top of Knockbrack is visible in its prominent position overlooking both this site and the passage-tomb cemetery at *Knockbrack/ Kitchenstown*. To the south there are uninterrupted views over the city as far as the Dublin/Wicklow Mountains. Looking south-east Howth seems to actually sit on the land like a low hill, an effect that can be seen from many sites. One has to wonder if it was a conscious effect on the builders' behalf or if it is just a coincidence of geography.

Mini-Gazetteer: 1.8km N there is a passage-tomb cemetery at *Knockbrack/ Kichenstown*. 6.1km NW there is a passage tomb at Fourknocks (Co. Meath). 9km NNE there is a passage tomb at Knocknagin (Co. Meath). 13.4km N there is a mound at Laytown (Co. Meath).

A gnarled thorn tree marks the position of the Hollywood Great mound

Howth Demesne
Portal Tomb
OS Sheet 50: O 277 383

Directions: *Park at Howth Castle golf course. Walk to the right of the clubhouse and follow the edge of the course until a track enters into the woods. The tomb is 50m along this track. Alternatively, if there are people playing golf, it may be safer to enter the rhododendron gardens and follow the muddy path through the trees to the right. Eventually you will reach a gravel path leading off to the right. The portal tomb is at the far end of this path.*

It is hardly surprising that this portal tomb has collapsed because of the disproportionality of the capstone and the rest of the monument – the chamber and portal structure seem far too flimsy to hold such a massive slab of rock. What is surprising is that so many people walk right past it every day while playing golf and do not know it exists, or don't even think twice about it whilst walking from one green to the next tee. These golfers probably only encounter it when a ball goes astray and then stumbling through undergrowth they come upon what is probably nothing more to them than a large, irregular pile of rocks. I hope when this does happen, the 35 ton cap stone and the 2m tall portal stones, one of which leans to the side dramatically, make them stop and wonder. Also, few of the people who take a walk through the neglected rhododendron garden of Howth Castle will visit it, due to it being located down an overgrown and waterlogged path.

Howth Demesne portal tomb. The two upright stones to the left are a portal stone and a doorstone. To the right of these is the other portal stone, which is leaning to one side

It is hard to make out the original form of the chamber, but I think it must have belonged to the family of tombs common to this area as also found at **Kilmashogue** (Larch Hill Scout Camp) and Onagh, just over the Wicklow border. These have a large box-form chamber made from three slabs. This one would have been a huge 2m square in plan. The door stone is three quarter height.

The 3.0m wide, 2.5m deep and 1.2m thick capstone is, like the other stones that make up the tomb, selected from the multitude of rocks that have fallen from the sheer cliff face of Muck Rock, just 40m away. This is, unusually, an uneven granite and quartz conglomerate, which gives the tomb a very rough and almost warty appearance – the other Dublin portal tombs are all Wicklow granite. Only the door stone and the inner faces of the portal stones are not rough. These may have been artificially smoothed or at least chosen for this property. All of the stones chosen have large veins or lumps of quartz in them. The face of Muck Rock, which the tomb looks directly onto, is also riddled with quartzite deposits and the early morning and late evening sun, light it up spectacularly. One can imagine that this was kept clear of interfering vegetation to enhance this effect.

One piece of folklore attached to this tomb is that it is the grave of Aideen, one of the daughters of Aengus of Ben Edar (Howth). She is said to have died of grief after her husband was killed in battle in 284 CE. Due to the tomb dating from 2000 BCE this story is obviously totally inaccurate and is more likely a perversion of the older Celtic myth of Edair, after whom Howth gets its Irish name, Ben Edair.

Left: Kill of the Grange bullaun stone, with the old church beyond

Opposite: Plan of Kilakee wedge tomb. *(After Healy)*

Mini-Gazetteer: 700m S there is a cairn at **Dunhill**. 1.7km NNW there is a mound at **Sutton South**. 6.4km NW there is a mound at **Drumnigh**. 12.2km S there is a passage tomb at **Dalkey Hill**.

Kill of the Grange
Bullaun Stone
OS Sheet 50: O 226 272

Directions: *The old church is located on St Fintan's Park, off Abbey Road. The bullaun stone is 50m in front of the entrance to the walled enclosure surrounding the church.*

Fifty metres in front of the walled enclosure, next to a low wall and usually surrounded by litter, there is a very unassuming boulder. It is not until closer inspection that one sees the half-buried bullaun on the side facing away from the wall. This partially visible bullaun is approximately 20cm in diameter.

The stone has obviously been overturned at some point, perhaps by the Church to stop people practicing pagan rites here. Some reports indicate that there may be more than one bullaun in the stone.

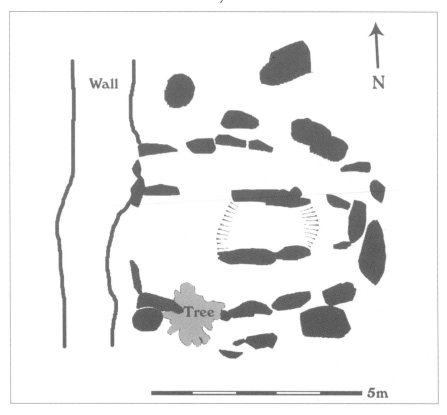

Mini-Gazetteer: 2.2km W there is a standing stone at **Leopardstown**. 4.9km SE there is a portal tomb at **Ballybrack**. 6.8km SSW there is a barrow and standing stone at **Newtown Hill**. 7.3km SSW there is a cairn at **Ballybetagh**.

Killakee
Wedge Tomb
OS Sheet 50: O 124 233

Directions: *Park at the small Massey Woods car park 200m west of the Hellfire Club Hill car park. Enter the woods and walk down to the bottom of the hill and find the bridge across the stream. Continue on and walk up the first track on the right. Near to the top of the hill a wall comes from the right to meet the track. At this point walk to the left at a 45-degree angle to the track until you find a holly tree next to a low wall. The tomb is on the opposite side of this wall.*

This small wedge tomb is difficult to find as it lies under a tree and is on the other side of a dry-stone wall to the direction from which you would usually approach. Its kerb measures about 5m across and still has many stones in place, but

The Druids' Judgement Seat

the cairn stone infill has mainly disappeared, leaving just low skeletal remains. It is very similar in plan to two of Dublin's other wedge tombs at Ballyedmonduff and Kilmashogue, but on a smaller scale.

The stones forming the walls of the 4m long gallery are nearly all present, as are those of the gallery's outer double walling. There is a 1m wide gap between the gallery walls and the double walling. Two large stones set to the front of the gallery appear to be the remnants of a façade.

Depending upon when you visit this site, it can be in any one of a number of states. In the autumn and winter it is often covered with leaves and even harder to locate. In the summer it can also be hidden, as it is sometimes covered with branches and made into a den by local children.

Mini-Gazetteer: 1.4km NNE there is a portal tomb at *Mount Venus*. 3km ENE there is a wedge tomb at *Kilmashogue*. 5km E there is a standing stone at *Ticknock*. 7.3km ESE there is a standing stone at *Glencullen*.

Killiney
The Druids' Judgement Seat
Passage Tomb
OS Sheet 50: O 255 247

Directions: *Head north on the Ballybrack-Killiney road and just after passing the Martello tower in Killiney turn left into Killiney Avenue. Continue over the junction at the end, turn into the first road on the right and park. Next to the junction you will see a little path disappearing into the trees and this is where you will find this odd monument.*

Known as The Druids' Judgment Seat this seems to be a bit of an embarrassment to the city of Dublin and its antiquarians. There was once a cairn here with three passage or portal tombs and many stones once lay scattered about bearing rock art. Nearby testament is paid to this site by a house called 'Druids' Hill' and another strangely named 'Stonehenge'.

In the late eighteenth century, presumably when some of the nearby houses were being built, a cemetery of stone-lined graves was uncovered, but I cannot find out if these were long cists or early Christian burials. Either is possible, as just 500m away is the sixth-century monastic site of Cill Inion Leinin (the church of the daughters of Leinin).

The reason I say that this monument seems to be somewhat of an embarrassment is because it was destroyed in the 1800s and turned into the strange perversion that you see today. Several stones from the passages have been reassembled to form a seat, hence its colloquial name. A further impression of shame is added by the fact that it is un-signposted and hidden away in a little grove, seemingly left untended and unvisited.

The seat is surprisingly comfortable. Sitting in it feels very odd indeed due to it now being faced by a high wall just 3m away, and the fact that you are conscious of its role in history. At one time there would have been extensive views over Dalkey Island to the north-east, so that the summer solstice sun would have risen above the island, an obvious reason for the original selection of this location. To the rear of the seat is a pair of large slabs, possibly the only part of the monument still in its original position, one of which has been carved and shaped to look like three stones. This has a drill hole in the centre of each 'pseudo-stone' that would indicate that it only just escaped being dynamited itself.

I think this monument is one of Dublin's greatest losses. Add to that the fact that it had three chambers and you get a site that was once of immense significance.
Mini-Gazetteer: 1.4km S there is a portal tomb at ***Ballybrack***. 5.3km SSW there is a wedge tomb at ***Carrickgollogan***. 7.8km WSW there is a wedge tomb at ***Ballyedmonduff***. 9.7km W there is a portal tomb at ***Taylorsgrange***.

Kilmashogue portal tomb from the south-east. The upright portal stone can be seen to the right, with the capstone behind it

Kilmashogue
Portal Tomb
OS Sheet 50: O 147 238

Directions: *This tomb is situated in the grounds of Larch Hill Scout Camp. This means that you will need an appointment to visit it.*

This tomb is more usually known as Larch Hill portal tomb; because it is located on the grounds of the scout camp that now occupies the land where Larch Hill House, the summer home of a wealthy Dublin businessman, once stood; reputedly the first place in Ireland where the British larch tree was planted. However, it is located in Kilmashogue townland and so should, by rights, be referred to as such.

This is probably the most ruinous of Dublin's portal tombs, but its size alone makes it worth a visit. The only stone that can really be said to stand properly is one of the portals, the other lies, broken, to one side of the capstone. This remaining portal stone is 3.5m tall and has an imposing presence. At its base lies what appears to be a low sill stone, a very unusual feature in a portal tomb, indicating that it may not have had a door stone normally found in this type of monument.

Behind this, covered by the huge capstone, are the stones that once formed the now flattened remains of a cubic chamber, implying it was of similar design to Howth and Onagh/Glaskenny (Co. Wicklow). These three stones are all slabs measuring 1.8m in length and would have stood 1.4m high.

Several other stones that look as if they were once part of the structure, lie scattered around, but it is impossible to say where in the structure they originate from. Lying nearby beneath the roots of a tree is a slender stone that is probably the missing portal stone. It is possible that it may have represented a degenerate courtyard at the front of the east-facing entrance.

This tomb is built on an outcrop of bedrock, around which a small stream runs. There are no signs of any cairn surviving, but the close proximity of the stream, to the rear of the chamber, makes it unlikely that there ever was a cairn.

Mini-Gazetteer: 1.5km S there is a cairn at **Tibradden**. 4.3km SW there is a stone circle at **Glassamucky Brakes**. 5.6km W there is a mound called **Knockanteedan** at **Glassamucky**. 8.9km W there is a barrow and cist at Lugmore.

Kilmashogue
Stone Pair
OS Sheet 50: O 138 249

Directions: *Take the R116 south from Dublin and turn left onto the R113. The stones are in a field to the left after a distance of about 200m, but are difficult to spot over the wall whilst in motion. Parking is also tricky and is best done around the corner near to the Kilmashogue standing stone. It is a dangerous road though and great care must be taken when walking along it.*

These stones present a bit more of an enigma than is usual. As well as the two stones at this location there is another standing stone 300m away on the same alignment – was this a much longer row? Along the walls of the field are many tall stones that once marked gateways, which look as if they may have been taken from the row.

These two stones are very well matched; both are square in section and around 1.8m tall. The one standing farthest from the road twists as it rises, making it seem as if it has been screwed into the ground.

Not surprisingly, this location offers a fine view of Howth in Dublin Bay.

Mini-Gazetteer: 1.1km W there is a portal tomb at **Mount Venus**. 2.6km WSW there is a standing stone and passage tomb at **Montpelier**. 4.6km SSW there is a bullaun stone at **Glassamucky Mountain**. 6.5km WSW there is a stone circle at **Belgard Deer Park**.

The north-western stone of Kilmashogue stone pair. The other stone is at the top of the field

Kilmashogue
Standing Stone
OS Sheet 50: O 154 245

Directions: *Take the R116 south from Dublin and turn left onto the R113. Take the first right and park near to the first large house on the left. The stone can be seen from the road level, with the driveway entrance on the far side of the field.*

This stone could be an extension of the Kilmashogue stone pair, but the stones are too different for this to be so (see previous site). The other stones are both square in section while this one is more rounded. The two sites are not inter-visible due to several walls built in-between them, but they do seem to be inline with each other.

At just 1.4m tall and leaning to the south it doesn't make a very impressive site on its own, but we must be thankful that it still exists at all.

Mini-Gazetteer: 3.9km SSE there is a cairn at **Tibradden**. 4.3km SW there is a standing stone at **Piperstown**. 5.6km SE there is a wedge tomb at **Ballyedmonduff**. 7.7km SW there is a passage-tomb cemetery and cairn at **Seahan**.

Kilmashogue standing stone

Kilmashogue
Wedge Tomb
OS Sheet 50: O 152 245

Directions: *From the R113 in south Dublin follow the signs for the Wicklow Way and park in the car park at O 150 245. There are some steps in the car park that lead onto the track above. Directly above these steps there is a path leading up into the trees. This tomb is about 50m up this track.*

The well-trod Wicklow Way passes just 50m from this tomb and yet there are no signposts to it. Sadly this means that it gets far fewer visitors than it deserves. Despite being quite ruinous it has a lot to offer and a well thought-out sign could alert the visitor to its presence quite easily. The information sign next to the path is badly damaged. Perhaps if the tomb received more visitors it might encourage authorities to replace it.

The area that was once covered by the round cairn is still mapped out by much of the kerb. Inside this area there is a thin spreading of cairn material. Originally this would have covered the entire tomb.

The main burial chamber is 4m long and 1.5m wide. It is defined by the remnants of its triple walling – that is to say that three parallel lines of orthostats formed each wall. The entrance to this gallery, marked by two well-matched

The gallery of Kilmashogue wedge tomb from the east

stones, looks to the west and faces the now almost non-existent Montpelier passage tombs on Hell Fire Club Hill.

Some time after its creation three further burials were placed in the cairn in the form of cist graves. One of these is a particularly fine example, the capstone of which is pushed aside allowing the visitor to see how the burial chamber below was constructed – four rectangular shaped slabs form the walls of this 1m square chamber. The second is 2m away and hidden by its capstone. The third was found in the ante-chamber of the gallery. This was a polygonal cavity, walled with loose stones. All three cists contained burial urns.

Mini-Gazetteer: 2.8km SE there is a standing stone at **Ticknock**. 3km WSW there is a wedge tomb at **Killakee**. 5.8km SW there is a portal tomb at **Cunard**. 8.2km E there is a passage tomb at **Ballymaice**.

Kiltiernan Domain
Portal Tomb
OS Sheet 50: O 198 224

Directions: *From the N11 take the R116 through Kiltiernan. There is a sharp left-hand bend with a cul-de-sac continuing straight ahead. Take this road. Turn left just before the ruined church and follow the road around until you come to a farm track on*

Kiltiernan Domain portal tomb from the south-west

the right. Park here and walk around the track, through one gate and past a yellow wall.
The dolmen is set on the side of the hill, protruding through the gorse just beyond the
yellow wall.

Kiltiernan Domain portal tomb is one of the largest in the country, with the
capstone measuring over 6m in length and up to 1.6m thick at its deepest point.
This huge capstone weighs over a colossal 35 tons and its long proportions give
the tomb a chamber that is 3m x 2m x 1.5m. The only downside to this wondrous
monument is that it was badly reinforced by a very ugly concrete pillar, which is
far too obvious. These supports were purposely made to not look like an original
part of the monument, which is understandable, but surely it could have been
done in a more subtle manner.

The tomb is situated on the west slope of a small hill, surrounded by gorse
bushes, facing west towards Two Rock Mountain and is, for most of the year,
almost completely hidden from view, only the 4m high point of the capstone
giving away its location. Its design and construction are very similar to that of
Brennanstown, just 3.6km away.

The portal stones are extremely difficult to see as the gorse usually grows right
up to the front, but they are an evenly-matched pair with a door stone standing
between them. The chamber is open at the sides, the stones probably having been
stolen away either to gain access or for building material. This is why the concrete support was added to it. What does remain of the chamber walls are small
stones, which when viewed from the side make the tomb look like a multi-legged

Kingswood mound in Ballymount Park

monster ready to pounce. This effect is further enhanced by the fact that the weight of the capstone has pushed all of its supporting stones forward.

Several stones lying to the rear of the tomb appear to be displaced stones that once formed part of the chamber. If this is the case then the slope of the capstone, a strong characteristic of portal tombs, was created wholly through the stone's wedge-shaped profile, as at **Glendruid**.

This tomb and that at **Brennanstown**, share so many characteristics that it would seem safe to assume that it was the same group of people who constructed them. The large capstones of both tombs share not only the same wedge-shaped profile and scale, but also the same diamond-shaped plan. The chambers are of similar proportions and the stones lying to the rear of Kiltiernan may also have been a small court-type feature, although the proximity of the bank here makes this very unlikely.

Mini-Gazetteer: 1.6km SSW there is a cairn at **Newtown Hill**. 3.6km ENE there is a portal tomb at **Brennanstown**. 7.4km S there is a rock-art panel at Onagh (Co. Wicklow). 10.2km SSE there is a barrow at Ballyremon Commons (Co. Wicklow).

Kingswood Mound
OS Sheet 50: O 089 305

Directions: *To reach Ballymount Park take the Ballymount exit from the M50 and head away from the city. Turn right just after the Luas station and then turn right again just*

The two Knockbrack monuments

before the shops. The estate is a bit of a maze, so it may be necessary to ask for directions to the park. Once in the park look for a castle tower between the M50 and the Luas line. The mound is 150m NW from this tower.

Set in the lovely Ballymount Park this mound seems to have had a varied history. At one point a structure was built upon it, which is possibly somehow connected with the nearby ruined tower now trapped between the Luas line and the M50 motorway. The mound is much older, though. It is 4m high and 20m in diameter.

Mini-Gazetteer: 4.5km NNE there is a kist at **Knockmaree**. 6.9km SSE there is a portal tomb at **Mount Venus**. 7.4km S there is a mound at **Glassamucky**. 8.7km SW there is a standing stone at **Raheen**.

Knockbrack/Kitchenstown
Passage tombs
OS Sheet 43: O 155 597

Directions: *From Naul head south on the R108 towards Ballyboghil. After 1.5km turn left at the crossroads. Continue for another 1.5km until you see a large area on the right-hand side of the road with a well-defined track running up the hill from the gate below. Walk up this track and head to the left where it forks and continue on into the next field. Here you will find three of the mounds. There are more on the other side of the hedge just below the mounds.*

On the northern slopes of Knockbrack lie five mounds. Three of these are in Kitchenstown TD and two are in Knockbrack TD. The hedgerow that

Knocken cairn from the coast road

separates the two groups actually forms the townland boundary. The Kitchenstown mounds are very scrappy and covered in gorse bushes. Those in Knockbrack are also covered in gorse bushes, but are much more impressive than those in the neighbouring field, with the largest being over 3m tall. The smaller mound in Knockbrack is 8m in diameter and just over 2m tall.

There is a sixth mound on the summit of the hill, also in Knockbrack TD, which cannot really be considered as part of the main group. Aerial photographs of the hill revealed that a large earthwork once surrounded this mound. This has since been ploughed flat leaving only a crop mark to commemorate its presence. This may be a hill fort, which is the official interpretation, or it may be a henge. Several other hills with passage tombs, such as Tara (County Meath) and Dun Ailinne (County Kildare), have henge-like earthworks and are thought to have been ceremonial centres. Perhaps Knockbrack was once such a place.

Across the valley to the north-east is the important passage-tomb cemetery at Fourknocks (Co. Meath), which along with this complex forms part of the chain of monuments that line the Delvin River.

Mini-Gazetteer: 1.8km S there is a mound at ***Hollywood Great***. 5.6km NW there is a mound at Herbertstown. (Co. Meath). 7.6km NNE there is a passage-tomb cemetery at ***Bremore***. 18.5km N there is a stone row at Baltray (Co. Meath).

Knockmaree cist in Phoenix Park

Knocken
Cairn
OS Sheet 43: O 230 610

Directions: *Head west from Skerries on the R127. There is a track and a gate 400m from the town on the left-hand side of the road. The cairn can be seen from this gate, some 50m away, at the top of the field.*

This coastal cairn has suffered the ravages of the agriculture industry. Although visible from the coast road there is not a lot of it left. The stones that make up its structure are entirely covered in grass. The cairn is about 5m in diameter and a little over 1m high.

Mini-Gazetteer: 2.8km W there is a standing stone at **Balrothery**. 6.9km SE there is a passage tomb, in poor repair, at **Knocklea**. 10.8km W there is a barrow at **Westown North**. 12.1km W there is a passage tomb at Fourknocks (Co. Meath).

Knockmaree – Phoenix Park
Kist
OS Sheet 50: O 106 347

Directions: *Enter Phoenix Park via the entrance near St Mary's Hospital on the south side. Drive around the park clockwise for just 400m. At the top of a bank to the right of the road, is a bungalow and the tomb is to the east of this, right next to the outer fence.*

With the comparatively recent development and artificial landscaping of Phoenix Park it is very difficult to assess the original position of this diminutive monument in the landscape. For a start it is not even certain that the tomb is in its original location – was it perhaps moved to make way for the house that now occupies the top of this low knoll?

The structure underwent some poor and careless repairs in 1973. The capstone has two cracks running through it, which have been cemented back together. This cup-marked stone is wonderfully kidney-shaped, but the dip in the one side may be due to a piece of it having been broken away. To add to the cemented cracks, there is also a square concrete pillar, which supports one corner. The unsightliness of this pillar makes it clear that it is definitely not part of the original structure.

The mound that covered this burial chamber was demolished in 1838. Apart from the central burial, which contained the skeletons of three people, there were also four later cists inserted into the mound. In 1959 a Bronze Age settlement was identified in the vicinity of Knockmaree, which could be related to the secondary cists.

When looking at the area on the OS map it is quite clear what attracted the builders to the vicinity, because this is overlooking the point where the River Liffey broadens before heading out to sea. Its location is also surprisingly high up, which provides views right across the city to the Dublin/Wicklow Mountains. The two larger monuments on **Seahan** can easily be made out, as can the cairn on Seefingan (County Wicklow) and the **Ticknock** passage tomb on Two Rocks Mountain.

Mini-Gazetteer: 1.7km WNW there is a barrow at **Palmerstown Lower**. 2.5km ENE there is a kist at **Dublin Zoo**. 4.5km SSW there is a mound at **Kingswood**. 10.2km SSE there is a portal tomb at **Mount Venus**.

Laughanstown
Wedge Tomb
OS Sheet 50: O 234 229

Directions: *At the time of writing the tomb is only accessible by crossing the fields from Tully church, but it will be accessible via the Cherrywood M50 spur once the building work around the site is completed. It is located alongside the Cherrywood junction in the southwest corner of the field/building site.*

There isn't a lot to be seen here other than a low, rectangular bump in a field. The site was excavated, but the stones were re-covered afterwards.

The site's location is quite interesting, being between the two ancient churches of Rathmichael and Tully, both of which are worth a visit. Tully has two fine crosses and Rathmichael has a fine set of grave slabs with a style of decoration peculiar to the area. The two churches are obviously much younger than the

Leopardstown standing stone

tomb, but their presence here does add a little weight to the importance of this area around the Loughlinstown river, which goes on to pass close to the portal tombs at Kiltiernan and Ballybrack.

Due to the motorway extension, extensive archaeological investigations were undertaken around this site, but as yet the findings haven't been made public. The Cherrywood M50 spur now passes just 50m or so from the site and soon it will be engulfed in a new development. At the time of writing the ground around it has been cleared for building. All of the beautiful views once enjoyed from here will be gone.

Mini-Gazetteer: 1.4km NNW there is a portal tomb at **Brennanstown**. 3.1km S there is a wedge tomb at **Carrickgollogan**. 5.7km SSW there is a kist at Parknasilog (Co. Wicklow). 9.1km S there is a standing stone at Kilmurry (Co. Wicklow).

Leopardstown
Standing Stone
OS Sheet 50: O 204 270

Directions: *The easiest way to access this site is via a style at the end of Leopardstown Oaks at the rear of the Leopardstown Inn on Brewery Road.*

This 1m tall stone has been the cause of some debate: is it a standing stone or is it the remnants of a wall or gate related to the old convent that once stood here?

The edge of the barrow at Lugg

It is my opinion that it is entirely genuine, and the factor that swung it for me is its proximity to an outcrop of bedrock just a few metres away.

The presence of this standing stone was only made widely known when developers threatened the site and it was mentioned in one of the objections made at the planning stage. When you enter the playing field you can't help but feel a little sorry for this diminutive stone standing all on its own.

Mini-Gazetteer: 3km SE there is a standing stone at ***Brennanstown***. 4.8km WSW there is a portal tomb at ***Taylorsgrange***. 9.5km WSW there is a passage tomb at ***Montpelier***. 10km SW there is a bullaun stone at ***Glassamucky Mountain***.

Lugg
Barrow Cemetery
OS Sheet 50: O 031 239

Directions: *An OS map and some determination are essential in the quest to find this site.*

In fields to the south of the pine plantation that surround ***Lugg*** henge, there is a barrow cemetery. Most of the barrows have been ploughed almost to ground level, but one, set high above the others, is in better condition. This exists as a 1m high, 15m diameter platform.

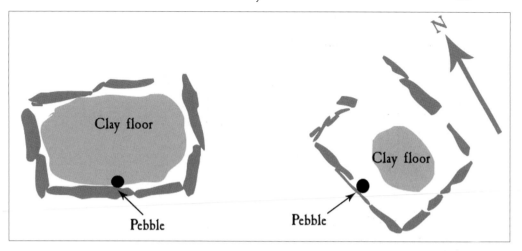

Plans of hearths from Lugg henge. (*After H.E. Kilbride-Jones*)

Mini-Gazetteer: 700m N there is a henge at **Lugg**. 1.7km SW there are two passage tombs at **Slievethoul**. 7.9km ESE there is a standing stone at **Piperstown**. 10km WSW there is a henge and standing stone at Forenaghts Great (Co. Kildare).

Lugg
Henge
OS Sheet 50: O 032 246

Directions: *The henge is hidden in the woods to the east of Saggart golf course. It is marked on the OS map with a red circle.*

Unless you can make out what lies beneath your feet a visit here could be a little disappointing, because the remains are in a clearing in a pine plantation and are overgrown. It is still possible to see the bank and ditch of the henge though, and by scrambling into the birch trees and gorse bushes you can find the smaller internal ditch that once surrounded a central mound.

The site was excavated in the 1950s prior to the trees being planted around it. It was found that the site had three phases, the last of which is the 35m diameter henge that is visible today. The middle phase was one of settlement, with small huts and hearths scattered across the site. The first phase was a 'sanctuary' structure, similar to a stone circle, but constructed with tree trunks rather than stones. This type of monument is rare in Ireland, with others having been identified at Navan Fort, County Armagh, and on the Hill of Tara, County Meath.

Above: The kerbstones of the larger tomb on Montpelier

Left: Montpelier standing stone looking towards the nearby passage tombs

Mini-Gazetteer: 2.7km E there is a cist at Lugmore. 2.3km SW there are two passage tombs at **Slievethoul**. 4.8km NW there is a barrow at **Athgoe Hill**. 9.3km SSE there is a passage tomb at Seefin (Co. Wicklow).

Montpelier
Passage Tomb
OS Sheet 50: O 115 237

Directions: *Follow the R115 south from Dublin and park in the car park at O121 237 (there is a big sign saying 'Hell Fire Club'). Right by the entrance to the car park there is a path leading up the hill, follow this to the top. The passage tombs are at the rear of the ruined building on the top of the hill.*

As you drive around the M50 it is hard not to notice the Hell Fire Club building upon the top of Montpelier, a hill more commonly known as the Hell Fire Club. This old hunting lodge is built with stones taken from the cairns of two passage tombs, the remains of which can just about be discerned on the ground as earthworks to the rear of the building. The easiest outline to trace is a circular bank about 15m in diameter and up to 2m high, with a dip at its centre, which is presumably where the chamber used to be. The large stones that can be seen around the southern edge of the larger mound are kerbstones. In the centre of the dip there are several stones that probably came from the chamber or passage.

The smaller mound is just 1m high and has an Ordnance Survey triangulation point mounted on it.

There are many ghostly stories associated with the lodge. A lot of the happenings are said to be caused by the anger of the Little People whose house was destroyed to make way for the construction of the lodge. The lintel over the fireplace in the lodge is said to have been a standing stone taken from the hill 100m south of the passage tombs.

Mini-Gazetteer: 1.8km SSW there is a group of cairns at **Piperstown**. 2.6km ESE there is a stone pair at **Kilmashogue**. 4km W there is a stone circle at **Belgard Deer Park**. 8km ESE there is a cairn, barrow and standing stone at **Newtown Hill**.

Montpelier
Standing Stone
OS Sheet 50: O 115 236

Directions: *Follow the R115 south from Dublin and park in the car park at O121 237 (there is a big sign saying 'Hell Fire Club'). Right by the entrance to the car park there is*

Mount Venus in 1851

a path leading up the hill, follow this to the top. The standing stone is on the far side of the ruined building on the top of the hill.

This fallen standing stone is on the top of the hill just 50m from the largest of the Montpelier passage tombs. It is sharply pointed and would not have stood much more than 1m tall. With the trees looming over it to the south and west, it is impossible to tell if the stone marked any significant alignments when viewed from the nearby tombs.

Mini-Gazetteer: 3.8km ENE there is a wedge tomb at **Kilmashogue**. 5km W there is a cairn and mound at **Ballymana**. 9.4km ESE there is a cairn at **Ballybetagh**. 9.8km W there are two passage tombs at **Slievethoul**.

Mount Venus
Portal Tomb
OS Sheet 50: O 127 247

Directions: *Directions to this tomb are hard to give at the time of writing, because there is some building work currently underway near to the site. From Oldbawn take the R113 towards Rockbrook/Woodtown until you come to a T-junction. Turn left and then take the first right on to Mount Venus Road. After about 500m you will come to the Dublin SPCA car park on the left-hand side of the road. The tomb is 150m beyond this, behind a wall. It is quite hard to spot as it is so overgrown most of the time.*

Another of County Dublin's hidden secrets, this collapsed portal tomb raises some questions: the main one being – was it ever finished? All that remains now is an enormous capstone propped up by a single portal stone, with the second lying on the ground close by. Unfortunately, this large tomb stands in a very overgrown and crowded walled area, which prevents you from standing back and taking it all in. The back edge of the large, 4m by 2.5m capstone rests on the ground and rises at a steep angle, giving it similarities to the huge portal tomb at Browne's Hill just outside of Carlow.

This is another one of those tombs that lies hidden away, with so few people ever learning of its existence. Its location is just 30m from the second tee on a golf course and yet, due to a wall and some trees, is totally hidden from the golfers.

The portal stones are very impressive; at least the one that still stands is – the other one is difficult to locate where it lies amongst the brambles and bracken. The remaining one stands some 2.5m tall and is a relatively slender 60cm x 60cm in section.

It was suggested by some that a large earthquake in the early 1800s was responsible for dislodging the capstone, but there is no documented, first-hand evidence for this.

Despite being located in Woodtown, the tomb gets its name from the large plantation house in whose grounds it once stood. There was a time when it was considered quite popular to have a dolmen in your garden.

Mini-Gazetteer: 1.4km SSW there is a wedge tomb at **Killakee**. 3.2km ENE there is a portal tomb at **Taylorsgrange**. 5.1km ESE there is a standing stone at **Ticknock**. 8.5km W there is a stone pair at **Boherboy**.

Mountseskin
Knockannavea
Cairn
OS Sheet 50: O 059 235

Directions: *From Brittas follow the signs for Bohernabreena along the R114. After 2km the road veers sharply left. Continue for a further 2km and take the second road on the left. This single-lane road rises and turns sharply. Continue until you reach the parking area near to some bungalows. Park here and walk along the track through the trees towards the small aerial at the top of the hill. The cairn is next to the aerial.*

As with many of the sites in the west Dublin Mountains this would be significantly better if pine plantations and aerials did not surround it. At first sight the cairn is quite well preserved, but a small portion of one side has been dug away and a field boundary crosses over another edge. The top has also been disturbed.

The cairn is 2.5m high and 20m in diameter. It occupies a position 200m west of the highest point on Tallaght Hill, which significantly reduces the views to the east. To the west you can see down the gentle western slopes of the hill

Knockannavea cairn on Tallaght Hill

Mountseskin mound from the west

Newtown Hill barrow from the north with the Great Sugar Loaf Mountain in the distance

and on to Saggart Hill, where more large masts and aerials identify where the two passage tombs are in **Slievethoul** TD. The pine forests on Saggart Hill prevent you from seeing the monuments on its southern end, such as the henge at Lugg.

At the time of writing the trees to the south had recently been felled, opening up magnificent views to Seahan and Seefin Mountains.

Knockannavea means 'the ravens' hill'.

Mini-Gazetteer: 2.8km WNW there is a henge at **Lugg**. 6.1km ESE there is a standing stone at **Piperstown**. 7.7km NNE there is a mound at **Kingswood**. 8.9km E there is a portal tomb at **Kilmashogue**.

Mountseskin
Mound
OS Sheet 50: O 051 235

Directions: *This mound is best appreciated from the road to its west. However, it can be reached by starting at Knockannavea cairn (see previous entry) and walking north, down through the woods.*

This mound, which is close to the site of a ploughed-out barrow cemetery, has been largely ploughed away. If the diameter of the remains is anything to judge by it would have been very large indeed.

The most spectacular thing about this site is the landscape that surrounds it. The fields gently slope away to the west and then rise up slightly before plunging into the Slade of Saggart. To the east Seahan and the Seefin Mountains rise up and dominate the site.

Mini-Gazetteer: 19.km E there is a passage tomb at **Ballymaice**. 3.5km W there are two passage tombs at **Slievethoul**. 5.9km ESE there is a cairn at **Piperstown**. 11.6km S there is a cairn at Sorrell Hill (Co. Wicklow).

Newtown Hill
Barrow
OS Sheet 50: O 193 212

Directions: *To reach Newtown Hill the best plan is to park at Johnny Fox's pub in Glencullen and walk east towards Kiltiernan until you reach the new church. To the east of the church there is a track alongside a bungalow that leads to a field. At the top of this field there is a gate that leads onto the top of the hill. The barrow is on the crest of the hill behind a hedge as you approach from this angle.*

The remains of Oissin's Grave on Newtown Hill

This is a fantastic example of a barrow and the finest of the many monuments that still remain on Newtown Hill. The mound seems to be undisturbed and the bank and fosse around are wonderfully well defined, except on the south side where a field boundary cuts through it. This barrow must have once been visible for miles around, but the same field boundary prevents it from appearing on the skyline.

The mound is approximately 10m in diameter and a little under 2m high from the base of the fosse, which is 1.5m broad. There is a standing stone 10m to the north-east (see next entry).

When considering this and the other monuments in the area – such as the **Glencullen** standing stone or the **Ballyedmonduff** wedge tomb – it is clear that this whole area has been occupied for large periods of time, possibly continuously since 3000 BCE.

Mini-Gazetteer: 2.4km NW there is a standing stone on Two Rocks Mountain at **Ticknock**. 4.4km ENE there is a wedge tomb at **Laughanstown**. 6.2km S there is a rock-art panel at Onagh (Co. Wicklow). 9.2km SSE there is a barrow at Ballyremon Commons (Co. Wicklow).

Newtown Hill
Oissin's Grave
Cairn
OS Sheet 50: O 191 210

Directions: *To reach Newtown Hill the best plan is to park at Johnny Fox's pub in Glencullen and walk east towards Kiltiernan until you reach the new church. To the east*

Newtown Hill hut site, looking towards the Great Sugar Loaf Mountain

of the church there is a track alongside a bungalow that leads to a field. At the top of this field there is a gate that leads onto the top of the hill. The cairn is towards the west end of the hill.

This cairn must have been huge, but it has been quarried to near non-existence. Even so, the remains are good enough to get a feel for what it might once have been like. The outer edges of the cairn still stand to a height of 1.5m in places, but this just hides the deep hole at its centre.

There is an unusual platform feature 10m from the cairn's south-eastern edge, which points towards the Great Sugar Loaf Mountain in County Wicklow. Was this constructed for observing the winter solstice sun setting behind the mountain?

Mini-Gazetteer: see Newtown Hill barrow.

Newtown Hill
Hut Site/Ring Cairn
OS Sheet 50: O 193 211

Directions: *The hut site is on the south-facing slopes, 75m from the Newtown Hill barrow (see previous entry).*

This monument consists of a double ring of stones, 15m in diameter, set 1m apart. This could either be the foundations for an Iron Age round house or the outer edge of a ring cairn. A third, slim possibility is that it is an embanked enclosure — a ritual site that is a cross between a henge and a stone circle.

Mini-Gazetteer: see Newtown Hill barrow.

Newtown Hill
Standing Stone
OS Sheet 50: O 193 212

Directions: *The standing stone is just 10m from the barrow described in the previous gazetteer entry.*

This standing stone is just under 1.5m tall and very rough, with no signs of having been shaped. When viewed from the north-east the top edge of the stone seems to echo the slopes of the Great Sugar Loaf Mountain in County Wicklow.

It is just possible that this stone marks the direction of the summer solstice sunrise from the barrow, but it is too close to the barrow to be sure without witnessing the event. The small wood to the east will probably be in the way too.

Mini-Gazetteer: see Newtown Hill barrow.

Newtown Hill
Stone Row
OS Sheet 50: O 192 212

Directions: *These stones are 50m west of the barrow in the adjacent field.*

There is actually a collection of stones lying around the two that remain standing, which could indicate that there was originally a stone circle here. Until the site is excavated, however, it has to be assumed that the row is the proper monument.

Each stone is 1m tall and shaped like a pointed egg. Their alignment is to the south-east and points directly towards the Great Sugar Loaf Mountain 9km away in County Wicklow.

Mini-Gazetteer: see Newtown Hill barrow.

Palmerstown Lower
Barrow
OS Sheet 50: O 088 353

Directions: *Stewart's Hospital is located just off the N4, 1km east of junction 7 on the M50. The barrow is located on a rise east of the hospital buildings, near to a car park.*

On the top of a ridge behind the Assisted Clinic at Stewart's Hospital there is a small, round copse. This is actually a tree-covered ring barrow. There is no mound, but the bank and ditch can be made out just inside the trees.

Above: Looking south past Newtown Hill standing stone towards the Great Sugar Loaf Mountain

Right: Newtown Hill stone row

The overgrown barrow at Palmerstown Lower

Piperstown standing stone, looking west over Glenasmole

Due to the buildings around the site it is not possible to appreciate what a wonderful location this really is, as it overlooks a very pronounced bend in the River Liffey to the east. As we know from Newgrange (County Meath) river bends were deemed sacred to many prehistoric peoples.

Mini-Gazetteer: 1.7km ESE there is a kist at *Knockmaree*. 4km E there is a kist at *Dublin Zoo*. 4.8km S there is a mound at *Kingswood*. 10.4km SSW there is a stone pair at *Boherboy*.

Piperstown
Standing Stone
OS Sheet 50: O 115 213

Directions: *Take the R115 south from Rockbrook and after about 4km you will see a turnoff to the right. Take this road and park on the left-hand side of the road wherever it is convenient after a distance of about 200m. To find the stone, walk west across the boggy hillside to the edge of the hill, where you should be able to see it.*

On one of my trips to try and locate the stone circle at Piperstown, I came across this lovely triangular-sectioned, 1.5m tall standing stone, which does not seem to appear in any of the records.

It stands on the edge of a plateau where there are traces of ancient houses and in view of the all but levelled cairns on Piperstown Hill. There are excellent views looking down the Dodder Valley and out over the Dublin plain to the north.

Further along the hill there are several other fallen stones, which could be part of an alignment that terminated with this stone at its most northern end. Further weight to this theory is added by the fact that the alignment would point straight at the stone circle at **Glassamucky Brakes**.

Mini-Gazetteer: 1.5km SSE there is a stone row at **Cunard**. 3.6km WSW there are three passage tombs and a cairn at **Seahan**. 6.6km WNW there is a cist at Lugmore. 10.6km ESE there is a kist at Parknasilog (Co. Wicklow).

Piperstown
Cairns and Settlement

Directions: *Take the R115 south from Rockbrook and after about 4km you will pass a turnoff to the right. Take this road for a little over 1km. You will pass a forest track on the right and see a parking area shortly afterwards on the left. Park here and walk west onto Piperstown Hill. The cairns are on the southern side of the hill and not too difficult to locate. Finding the hut circles is a little trickier.*

The Ordnance Survey map shows three cairns on the southern slopes of Piperstown Hill, only one of which is easily identifiable on the ground. The other two can be found, 30m down the hillside from this, by looking carefully for the large kerbstones that define their outlines. The identifiable cairn was reconstructed during the large-scale excavations that were undertaken here in 1962 after a fire stripped much of the peat and heather from the hillside in 1960.

Fifteen sites were identified, containing a mixture of burial cairns and habitation sites. The material of the small cairn mentioned above, labelled Site K on the excavation plans, was removed to reveal a small stone circle with a pit at its centre

The smallest of the cairns on Piperstown Hill

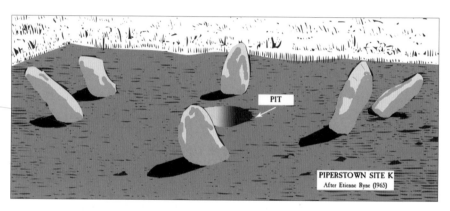

Piperstown Hill: the stone circle beneath Site K. *(After Rynne)*

Raheen standing stone from the west

that contained small amounts of cremated bone. The cairn was rebuilt over this, but the upright stones can be made out poking through.

A large collection of worked flints was collected during the excavations. Although no radiocarbon dating was undertaken on the cremated remains from the pit in Site K, the complex is believed to date from either the Late Neolithic or Early Bronze Age

There is some speculation about the accuracy of a number of the observations made during these excavations and the hillside has recently become the focus of another archaeological survey. It will be very interesting to compare the findings from this new survey with the original excavation plans.

On the top of the hill there are two small cairns, one of which is built on top of a pre-bog wall.

Mini-Gazetteer: 1.4km SE there is a stone circle at **Glassamucky Brakes**. 4.2km E there is a cairn at **Tibradden**. 7.5km WNW there is a stone pair at **Boherboy**. 8.9km SSW there is a barrow at Ballynabrocky (Co. Wicklow).

Raheen
Standing Stone
OS Sheet 50: O 038 234

Directions: *Take the N81 south from Dublin. Shortly after the junction with the N82 you will pass a hospital entrance. Take the next left just around the bend. Follow the road around to the right until you reach a large red gate on your right-hand side. Park here. If the gate is locked you may have to find the farmer. Follow the track until you see a barn on the right. Walk past this and through the next gate. The stone is then 40m to your left.*

This is the only standing stone in the area known to be decorated with rock art. One of its 1.3m broad faces has in excess of twenty small cup marks scattered over its lower half.

This is a rough looking stone with seemingly little elegance and stands on a westward-facing slope, uncomfortably close to a modern barn. Its size is impressive though, standing over 2m tall and over 1m thick, giving it an imposing presence.

Unfortunately, either due to the nature of the rock or by having been used as a rubbing post by cattle, the cup marks are worn away and require just the right light to see them all properly.

Mini-Gazetteer: 1.3km NNW there is a henge at **Lugg**. 4.5km SW there are two standing stones at Tinode (Co. Wicklow). 8.6km E there is a wedge tomb at **Killakee**. 10.8km SSW there is a standing stone at Knockieran (Co. Wicklow).

Rathmichael

Bullaun Stone
OS Sheet 50: O 239 219

Directions: *From Stepaside head south to Kiltiernan. Take the left turn after the Statoil garage (it may be best to zero your milometer at this junction.) Continue for 3km until you pass a few cottages on the left. On the right there is a rough farmtrack with a cul-de-sac sign – blink and you'll miss it! Drive up this track to the white gates and drive on to the church and park. Walk back down the lane until you reach a private driveway on the left. The bullaun stone is tucked away beneath the bushes on the opposite edge of the lane.*

Rathmichael church was built within an old fort and the bullaun stone probably pre-dates that. It is a large flat-topped stone set into the ground so that its upper surface is level with the laneway it stands beside. A single bullaun lies at roughly the centre of the stone, measuring 25cm in diameter and 15cm in depth.

Mini-Gazetteer: 2.1km S there is a wedge tomb at **Carrickgollogan**. 4.1km W there is a portal tomb at **Kiltiernan Domain**. 8km S there is a standing stone at Kilmurry (Co. Wicklow). 9.7km S there is a mound at Ballyremon Commons (Co. Wicklow).

Rush
Knocklea
Passage Tomb
OS Sheet 43: O 270 554

Directions: *Head north from Rush on the R128 for about 1km after a very sharp bend in the road in Rush. I found space to park in a new estate on the left, just opposite a farm track leading towards the sea. Follow this track until you reach the cliffs and the sea. Walk towards Howth until you reach the cliff top. That's where this tomb used to be!*

Almost nothing, if anything at all, remains of this coastal passage tomb. I have included it for completeness and for the fact that it adds a little weight to my theory that many of the monuments around Dublin were built to honour the islands off the coast of Dublin, i.e. Howth, Lambay and Ireland's Eye.

There is one large stone visible on this site now, which looks as if it was from the tomb's kerb. Looking south, over the beach below from the cliff top on which the tomb is situated, Lambay Island seems to float magically on the horizon. Lambay is an extinct volcano and the source of Lambay Porphyry, which was quarried and used to make polished stone axes.

Looking south over Seahan 1 towards Seefingan and Seefin

Mini-Gazetteer: 6.9km NW there is a cairn at **Knocken**. 8.9km NW there is a standing stone at **Balrothery**. 11.9km WNW there is a mound at **Hollywood Great**. 12.3km WNW there is a passage-tomb cemetery at **Knockbrack/Kitchenstown**.

Seahan 1
Passage Tomb
OS Sheet 56: O 081 197

Directions: *Follow the N81 from Dublin and turn left to Kilbride on the R759 and follow the signs to Sally Gap. Turn left at the next crossroads and then take the first right and drive to the T-junction by a bridge. Turn left (if the road is open) and then park in one of the entrances to a track on the right. Just keep walking up.*

This is the southernmost monument on the mountaintop. The cairn has been removed and just the stones defining the round chamber and short passage remain. A large, fallen slab across the entrance to the south-facing passage may be the original blocking stone.

The chamber is 2m in diameter. There is a large quartz boulder at its rear right-hand corner.

Just on the Wicklow/Dublin border two adjacent hills stand out: Seahan and Seefin. The main reason these are so prominent is that each peak is crowned by a passage tomb. Seahan also has the remains of a smaller tomb and another cairn, which may or may not be a second passage tomb. The proud rounded form of both of these mountains with their cairns look very breast-like when viewed from County Kildare to the west. It is hard to imagine that this is coincidental.

The cairn on Seahan from the south

Like all the other west Wicklow Mountain hill-top sites the climb is quite arduous, but the rewards of far-reaching views makes the effort worthwhile – on a clear day you can see as far as the Mournes and Slieve Gullion in Northern Ireland.

NB: The numbering system used here for the Seahan monuments is my own, running south-north.

Mini-Gazetteer: 3.5km NNE there is a mound at **Glassamucky**. 6km SSW there is a standing stone at Athdown (Co. Wicklow). 9.9km SW there is a passage tomb at Lugnagun (Co. Wicklow). 10.8km E there is a standing stone at **Glencullen**.

Seahan 2
Cairn
OS Sheet 56: O 081 197

Directions: *See Seahan 1*

This cairn is the largest monument on the mountaintop and is visible for miles around. It has never been opened and may contain a passage tomb. Early reports state that there was a kerb of large stones visible, but the cairn material has since slipped and buried these.

Looking south you have spectacular views that take in the cairn on Seefingan and the passage tomb on Seefin, both in County Wicklow.

The cairn is 25m in diameter and over 2m high. The Ordnance Survey have erected a triangulation point on top of it.

The chamber of Seahan 3 with Seahan 2 in the background

NB: The numbering system used here for the Seahan monuments is my own, running south-north.

Mini-Gazetteer: see Seahan 1

Seahan 3
Passage Tomb
OS Sheet 56: O 082 197

Directions: *See Seahan 1*

Of the four monuments on Seahan this is the most interesting. The grass-covered mound is 25m in diameter and 1.8m high. Much of the kerb is in place and visible. This is made of large slabs laid end to end set on edge. The largest of these is 2m long.

At some point an attempt to open the chamber was made and a roof slab and the tops of several orthostats from the chamber and passage are visible on the top, set slightly off centre. It is very difficult to be certain, but the passage may align to the north-west.

NB: The numbering system used here for the Seahan monuments is my own, running south-north.

Mini-Gazetteer: see Seahan 1

Left: The scant remains of Seahan 4

Below: Knockananiller from the south

Seahan 4
Passage Tomb
OS Sheet 56: O 082 197

Directions: *See Seahan 1*

This is the smallest and most run down of the monuments on the mountaintop. The few remaining orthostats only just protrude above the peat. The northern side of the west-facing passage is well-defined. A low sill stone can be seen separating the passage and the opening of the chamber.

This is an undifferentiated passage tomb, which means that the chamber is just a slight widening of the passage. The stones marking the rear of the chamber are either missing or still buried beneath the peat.

NB: The numbering system used here for the Seahan monuments is my own, running south-north.

Mini-Gazetteer: see Seahan 1

Slievethoul
Knockananiller
Cairn
OS Sheet 50: O 019 237

Directions: *The easiest way to reach this site is from the car park at grid reference O 024 235. From there walk up the track and continue over the first 'crossroads'. Continue until you reach a path on the right that runs alongside a fence. Take this path. After it crosses a gravel track make sure you are on the left-hand side of the fence. This path turns sharp left and takes you onto the top of the Knockananiller cairn.*

At the north end of Saggart Hill are two monuments that seem to be related. The major one of these is a huge cairn some 4m tall and 30m in diameter, which could be a passage tomb. The other is situated on the other side of a fence (see **Crockaunadreenagh**).

Both of these monuments overlook a round-topped spur known as Lugg, which is surely a reference to a Lugnassa link: perhaps there were once festivals held on the hill. A henge on the hill was excavated and given a very early date. This earthwork originally had a timber circle within it. Another link to Lugnassa and the Celtic god Lugh can also be attributed to this location. The sun rises on Lugnassa morning over Howth when viewed from this location.

This cairn is known as Knockananiller, which means the Mount of the Eagle.

Slievethoul 1 from the
north-west

Mini-Gazetteer: 4.5km NW there is a barrow at ***Athgoe Hill***. 6.4km ESE there is a barrow at ***Ballinascorney Upper***. 9.2km SE there is a passage tomb at Seefin Hill (Co. Wicklow). 10.3km WSW there is a standing stone at Baltracey (Co. Kildare).

Slievethoul 1
Passage Tomb
OS Sheet 50: O 017 228

Directions: *The best approach is to park at the entrance to a small track at O 014 225 and walk up the track. Take the first right-hand junction and follow the track around until you reach the radio masts. The tomb is situated to the left of the track behind what looks like an airfield control tower.*

Surrounded by over-bearing trees and tall, ugly radio and mobile phone masts this unassuming 3m high mound is another hidden treasure.

It is hard to make out more than just a small mound because of the rough scrub growth that covers most of it, but close inspection reveals a dip in the top where the roof has collapsed and some large stones on the west side that could mark the entrance.

It is unfortunate that the trees and masts block the views to the east, because these would be quite special taking in the northern edge of the Dublin Mountains.

The trees were felled to the west in 2006 and now most of this vista has been opened up. On a clear day you can look down onto Lyons Hill and Athgoe Hill and see right over the plains of Kildare.

This monument is also known as the Hill of the Herd Boy.

Mini-Gazetteer: 1.7km NE there is a henge at ***Lugg***. 4.9km E there is a cairn at ***Ballymana***. 8.3km WSW there is a henge and standing stone at Forenaghts Great (Co. Kildare). 10.3km SSW there is a standing stone at Burgage (Co. Wicklow).

The mound at Sutton
South from the beach

Slievethoul 2
Passage Tomb
OS Sheet 50: O 019 228

Directions: *The best approach is to park at the entrance to a small track at O 014 225 and walk up the track. Take the first right-hand junction and follow the track around until you reach the radio masts. There are two towers with microwave dishes on them. The tomb is 100m beyond the one on the right.*

Large quantities of the trees surrounding this monument were felled in 2006, making it quite easy to locate now. The bright green grass covering the 1m high remains of the cairn, contrasts with the havoc and destruction caused by the pine plantation.

The cairn is 25m in diameter and has a ditch surrounding it, but this may not be an original feature: it could be a by-product of the tree planting.

Mini-Gazetteer: see Slievethoul 1

Sutton South
Mound
OS Sheet 50: O 267 397

Directions: *This mound is in the garden of a private residence, but can be seen from the beach just off Burrow Road. Park on Burrow Road/Claremont Road and walk through to the beach.*

This beachside mound is in a private garden, the back wall of which cuts through the north side of it. A covering of shrubs and trees makes it impossible to see the monument clearly, but it appears to be around 4m high and 10-12m in diameter.

The Brehon's Chair at Taylorsgrange

Mini-Gazetteer: 1.7km SE there is a portal tomb at **Howth Demesne**. 2.3km SSE there is a cairn at **Dunhill**. 4.3km NW there is a mound at **Drumnigh**

Taylorsgrange
The Brehon's Chair
Portal Tomb
OS Sheet 50: O 158 255

Directions: *From junction 13 on the M50 take the road marked Rathfarnham. At the first major junction turn left and continue back under the motorway. The Brehon's Chair housing estate is on the right after 75m.*

When viewed for the first time the Brehon's Chair, as this tomb is called, is a mystifying monument, for all that remains of it are three monstrous stones forming a cove-like structure. These are, however, the door stone and portal stones of what must have once been among the largest portal tombs in the country. One of the portal stones now leans to the side slightly, but the other reaches an incredible 3.5m tall. With a capstone added it must have reached at least 5m tall. The larger of the portal stones must weigh in at 7 tons.

The door slab is nearly full height and one can imagine that, in its complete state, it would have resembled tombs like Gaulstown and Knockeen, both in County Waterford, and Haroldstown in County Carlow. All three of these have two capstones, rather than the usual one.

Located in the townland of Taylorsgrange this great spectacle is now, sadly, locked away in the grounds of a gaudily-painted private housing estate, behind a coded gate making access quite difficult. The M50 motorway passes just 20m to the east, and so, unless you can catch the gates open as someone leaves, the only access is via the college next door and over a low fence. It now seems to be used as a den for the children of the estate who play on the surrounding green and I have often found it strewn with toys and litter.

Brehon is another name for a head Druid and the name The Brehon's Chair was probably given to this monument in the late eighteenth or early nineteenth century, when all such monuments were being ascribed to the Druids. It was most likely considered to be the seat from which the chief Druid sat in judgment. It was very popular during this period to think of portal tombs as Druidical monuments and many are named 'The Druids' Altar' or something similar (see The Druids' Judgment Seat in Killiney).

When the M50 work was underway the area immediately surrounding this tomb was extensively excavated. The findings were very intriguing, showing that the site had gone through many phases of use. Cooking areas and hut sites surrounded the monument. Traces of the cairn were found during excavation, in which a later burial with a food vessel was inserted as a secondary burial.

Mini-Gazetteer: 2.1km WSW there is a stone pair at **Kilmashogue**. 4.6km WSW there is a standing stone and two passage tombs at **Montpelier**. 6.9km SW there is a portal tomb at **Cunard**. 9.9km ESE there is a portal tomb at **Ballybrack**.

Tibradden
Chambered Cairn
OS Sheet 50: O 148 223

Directions: *From Glencullen take the R116 north-west for around 6km until you reach the car park clearly marked Tibradden on the right-hand side of the road. Be warned: this car park is locked from 4pm. From there basically keep walking upwards and south around the winding track. Go to the first bend and double back, miss out on the next left track and then shortly after the next left angle turn right. You should be walking in between the plantation on your right and a fence on your left after about 200m. Keep on walking along this rocky path and it will take you straight to the cairn.*

For many years this was thought to be a passage tomb (it even gets a mention in Robert Graves' *The White Goddess* as such). However, it is simply a cairn that had a cist burial at the centre, which is now in The National Museum in Dublin. The cairn survives at a height of 2m, the middle of which has been removed to give a perfectly round, but false, chamber in the centre. This along

Looking over the cairn towards Howth

with the pseudo passage that can be seen, was created to facilitate easy access to the burial within.

The views from here are outstanding. The **Ticknock** passage tomb on Two Rocks Mountain lies to the east and Dublin opens up to the north. To the south and west lie the Wicklow Mountains.

Tibradden is derived from Tigh Brodhoin (the House of Brodhion) which could either mean that Brodhoin was buried in this cairn or that he lived in one of the other structures that were recorded on the hilltop by the Ordnance Survey in the early nineteenth century, but are no longer visible today.

One thing to note here is that the cairn does not occupy the highest point on the hilltop. It is positioned slightly to the north, which actually puts it in a position where Howth is not obscured by the slopes of Two Rocks Mountain. This positioning could be coincidental and due to other structures already occupying the highest point or it could indicate that a view of Howth was considered important by the builders.

Mini-Gazetteer: 2.2km N there is a wedge tomb at **Kilmashogue**. 3.5km WSW there is a standing stone at **Piperstown**. 5.8km ESE there is a cairn at **Ballybetagh**. 9.9km W there is a mound at **Mountseskin**.

Fairy Castle on Two Rocks Mountain from the west

Ticknock – Two Rocks Mountain
Fairy Castle
Passage Tomb
OS Sheet 50: O 172 224

Directions: *There are several ways to reach the top of Two Rocks Mountain. The most popular route is to park on Ticknock Road (off the R113 near to where it crosses the M50) and walk up. Another route is to park at the Kilmashogue car park on the Wicklow Way and walk across from there.*

The cairn on the peak of Two Rocks Mountain can be seen as a small bump for miles around. At just over 530m above sea level it is one of Dublin's highest monuments. Walkers have built a 'mini-cairn' on the flattened top of the original cairn alongside an Ordnance Survey trig point.

The entrance to the passage that was once described by locals as a 'cave' can no longer be seen, but a small depression on one side could represent where it is. The cairn is now only 1.5m high and approximately 20m in diameter. There are no kerbstones visible, but cairn material that has slipped or the peat that surrounds the monument, may be covering them.

As you would expect, the views from this vantage point are simply massive. All of Dublin is laid out before you and on a clear day you can see as far as the Mourne Mountains in County Down. It is quite easy to pick out Slieve Gullion to their west also. Looking south you can see right down the Wicklow Mountains.

Ticknock standing stone, looking out over Dublin Bay

Mini-Gazetteer: 2.4km ESE there is a standing stone at **Newtown Hill**. 2.8km NW there is a standing stone at **Kilmashogue**. 6.8km ESE there is a wedge tomb at **Carrickgollogan**. 11.1km SE there is a pair of cairns at Glencap Commons (Co. Wicklow).

Ticknock – Two Rocks Mountain
Standing Stone
OS Sheet 50: O 174 227

Directions: *This stone is 400m NNE of Ticknock passage tomb on the top of Two Rocks Mountain.*

This standing stone can be found on the east slopes of Two Rocks Mountain between the passage tomb at Ticknock and the granite tors of Three Rocks Mountain. It is slightly obscured by the peat and heather that covers these slopes.

The visible part of the stone is triangular and 1m high.

Mini-Gazetteer: 2.4km E there is a portal tomb at **Kiltiernan Domain**. 2.9km SE there is a standing stone at **Glencullen**. 6.6km W there is a cairn at **Piperstown**. 9.9km W there is a stone circle at **Belgard Deer Park**.

Westown North barrow from the south

Westown North
Barrow
OS Sheet 43: O 122 602

Directions: *Take the R122 from Naul following signs for Garristown for 1km. On the right-hand side of the road you will pass a garden centre. The barrow is in the field 100m past its entrance and can be seen from the road. The landowner does not often allow people to visit the site for insurance reasons.*

Echoing the tombs at Fourknocks (County Meath) on the north side of the Delvin Valley, this barrow is one of the finest in the country. It was built on a small spur of land to ensure maximum impact on passers-by. From the road it still looks massive, even with the trees and hedgerows surrounding it. The hedges are too high and too close to the monument to get a true feeling of how it would once have interacted with the landscape.

The mound is divided into levels with the lower level 1.5m high and 20m in diameter. The upper level is 1.5m high and about 8m in diameter.

Mini-Gazetteer: 3.4km NW there is a mound at Heathtown (Co Meath). 3.9km SE there is a mound at **Hollywood Great**. 10km ESE there are two henges on Windmill Hill (Co. Meath).

Acknowledgements

I need to thank a few people who have given me support and encouragement. Obviously, I have to give enormous credit to the patience of my family, because they have had to contend with me going out and visiting all the places mentioned herein and then shutting myself away to write about them. To them I can't say a large enough THANK YOU. My wife, Uta, has shown enormous patience while reading and rereading (not to mention rereading again) the manuscript to proofread it.

Anthony Weir has been a big inspiration to me and I have enjoyed his company on many trips. His website (www.irishmegaliths.org.uk) was a major source of information for me when I first started to rekindle my interest in megalithic monuments – his book *Early Ireland: A Field Guide* has been a great help to me as well. Furthermore, through Anthony's efforts I was inspired to create my own website (www.megalithomania.com), which deals with all ages and types of antiquity across Ireland and is now one of the largest sources of such information on the Internet. Further thanks go to the tens of thousands of people that regularly visit megalithomania.com.

The late T.C. Lethbridge whose works have shown me that you do not have to have an orthodox style or approach to your subject to write a good book also deserves a mention. Which leads me to – thanks to the editing team for putting up with me.

In relation to my website and some of the graphics in this book I have to make offerings before the altar to the artistic genius of Holy McGrail, who has helped me make megalithomania.com one of the best-looking sites on the web.

Everyone I know has been very supportive and, naturally, they deserve a 'thank you' as well.

A last little word must go to Julian Cope, who not only inspired me to resume visiting ancient monuments through his book, *The Modern Antiquarian*, but has also given me a great amount of personal encouragement regarding putting pen to paper to get this book written and other books started.

Bibliography

Abbreviations used:
JRSAI – *Journal of the Royal Society of Antiquaries of Ireland*
PRIA – Proceedings of the Royal Irish Academy

Aalen et al. *Atlas of the Irish Rural Landscape*, Cork, Cork University Press, 1997
Ball, Francis E. *A History of County Dublin*, Dublin, Greene's Bookshop, 1995
Beckensall, Stan. *British Prehistoric Rock Art*, Gloucestershire, Tempus, 1999
Bergh, Stefan. *Landscape of the Monuments*, Stockholm, University of Stockholm, 1995
Ua Broin, Liam. *Traditions of Drimnagh, Co. Dublin, and its Neighbourhood*, JRSAI vol. 72, pt. 3, 1942
Burenhult, G. *The Megalithic Cemetery of Carrowmore*, Sweden, Göran Burenhult, 2001
Burl, Aubrey. *Prehistoric Stone Circles*, Shire, Shire Publications Ltd, 1997
Burl, Aubrey. *The Stone Circles of Britain, Ireland and Brittany*, London, Yale University Press, 2000
Case, H. *Irish Neolithic Pottery: Distribution and Sequence*, London, Proceedings of the Prehistoric Society, vol. 27, 1961
Cleary, Cooney, Coles et al. *New Agendas in Irish Prehistory*, Dublin, Wordwell, 2000
Conney, G. *The Place of Megalithic Tomb Cemeteries in Ireland*, Cambridge, Antiquity Publications, Antiquity vol. 64, no. 245, 1990
Conolly, Michael. *Discovering the Neolithic in Kerry – A Passage Tomb at Ballycarty*, Dublin, Wordwell, 1999
Corlett, Christiaan. *Antiquities of Old Rathdown*, Dublin, Wordwell, 1999
Dames, Michael. *Mythic Ireland*, London, Thames & Hudson, 1992
Davis, M. *The Diffusion and Distribution Pattern of the Megalithic Monuments of the Irish Sea and North Channel Coastlands*, Antiquaries Journal, 1946
Evans, Estyn. *Prehistoric and Early Christian Ireland – A Guide*, London, Batsford, 1966
Fanning, Thomas. *A Wedge-Tomb at Laughanstown, County Dublin*, JRSAI, vol. 104, 1974
Flannagan, Laurence. *Ancient Ireland – Life Before The Celts*, Dublin, Gill & MacMillan, 1998
Handcock, William. *The History of Tallaght*, Dublin, Anna Livia Press, 1899
Harbison, Peter. *Guide to National and Historic Monuments of Ireland*, Dublin, Gill & MacMillan, 1992
Harbison, Peter. *Pre-Christian Landscapes*, London, Thames & Hudson Limited, 1988
Hartnett, P J & Eogan G. *Feltrim Hill, Co. Dublin: A Neolithic and Early Christian Site*, JRSAI, vol. 94, pt 1, 1964

Healy, Patrick. *An Unrecorded Wedge-Tomb At Killakee, County Dublin*, RSAI, vol. 108, 1978

Healy, Patrick. *Paddy Healy's Dublin*, online manuscript courtesy of South Dublin Libraries

Herity, Michael. *The Finds from the Irish Portal Dolmens*, JRSAI, vol. 94, pt 2, 1964

Herity, Michael. *Irish Passage Graves*, Shannon, Irish University Press, 1974

Herity, Michael (Editor). *Ordnance Survey Letters Dublin*, Dublin, Four Masters Press, 2001

Joyce, P W. *Irish Place Names*, Belfast, Appletree Press, 2006

Joyce, Weston St John. *The Neighbourhood of Dublin*, Dublin, M.H. Gill & Son, 1921

Keeling, David. *A Group of Tumuli and a Hill-Fort near Naul, County Dublin*, JRSAI, vol. 113, 1983

Kilbride-Jones, H E. *The Excavation of a Composite Early Iron Age Monument with 'Henge' Features at Lugg, County Dublin*, PRIA, vol. 53, no. 5, 1950

Kilbride-Jones, H E. *The Excavation of a Composite Tumulus at Drimnagh, County Dublin*, JRSAI, 1939

Kilbride-Jones, H E. The *Excavation of an Unrecorded Megalithic Tomb on Kilmashogue Mountain, County Dublin*, PRIA, vol. 56, no. 6, 1954

Liversage, G D. *Excavations at Dalkey Island, County Dublin, 1956-1959*, PRIA, 1968

MacNeill, Máire. *The Festival of Lughnasa*, Oxford, Oxford Universiy Press, 1962

McC Dix, E R. *Some Antiquities on Tallaght Hill*, RSAI, vol. 55, pt II, 1925

Mitchell, John. *Megalithomania*, London, Thames & Hudson, 1985

Mitchell, G F. *Further Excavations of the Early Kitchen-Midden at Sutton, County Dublin*, JRSAI, 1972

Mongey, L. *The Portal Dolmens of South-Eastern Ireland*, Waterford, Journal of the Waterford Spelaeological Society, vol. 1, 1941

Ó Nualláin, Seán. *Stone Circles in Ireland*, Dublin, Town House, 1995

Ó Ríordáin, Sean P. *Antiquities of the Irish Countryside*, 5th edn, London, Methuen, 1979

Ó Ríordáin, Sean P. & Ruaidhrí de Valera. *Excavation of a Megalithic Tomb at Ballyedmonduff, Co. Dublin*, PRIA, vol. 55, no. 3, 1952

O'Sullivan, Muiris. *Megalithic Art in Ireland*, Dublin, Town House, 1993

Raftery, Joseph. *Prehistoric Ireland*, London, Batsford, 1951

Rynne, Etienne. *Survey of a Probable Passage Grave Cemetery at Bremore, Co. Dublin*, JRSAI, vol. 90, pt 1, 1960

Rynne, Etienne & Patrick Healy. A *Group of Prehistoric Sites at Piperstown, County Dublin*, PRIA, vol. 64, no. 3, 1965

Watkins, Alfred. *The Old Striaght Track*, London, Methuen, 1925

Weir, Anthony. *Early Ireland – A Field Guide*, Belfast, Blackstaff, 1980

Oireachtas questions, March 28th 2006